MALE AND FEMALE: IDENTITY

EDITED BY *John Harrington*

University of Massachusetts

JOHN WILEY & SONS, INC.

NEW YORK • LONDON • SYDNEY • TORONTO

COVER PHOTOS: Leonard Freed, *Magnum;* Roger Malloch, *Magnum*

Library of Congress Cataloging in Publication Data

Harrington, John, 1942-   comp.
  Male and female: identity.

  (Perception in communication)
  1. Readers—Sex role. I. Title.
PE1127.S4H3   808.04'275   76-37433
ISBN 0-471-35262-4

Printed in the United States of America.

10 9 8 7 6 5 4 3 2 1

For Marie and Brendan

Series Preface

"Perception in Communication" is a series of brief topical readers presenting a collection of expository prose, verse, fiction, drama, and nonverbal media for the student of composition. No restrictive framework has been imposed on any of the volumes. If a common framework exists, it stems from the editors' emphasis on the principle of comparison and contrast and their mutual desire to make the questions and exercises participatory. The questions are focused on themes and matters of rhetorical technique that will provoke discussion between instructor and student in responses to the authors and editors.

Experience demonstrates that a student tends to write better when a timely, substantial subject engages his interest, or when the subject is elaborated and reviewed in a variety of modes of communication. Although the major emphasis of this series is on written communication, there are also a number of multimedia projects such as collages, comic routines, poems, dramatic productions, films, pictorial essays, posters, songs, and tapes. The editors use this multimedia material in such a manner that they are very definitely assignments in composition.

By acknowledging several modes of communication and encouraging experimentation in more than one, the editors recognize the heterogeneity of today's college audience and its various commitments, concerns, goals, and needs. It is the editors' belief that presenting these various modes of communication will engage not only the reader's mind but also his sensory perception.

CHARLES SANDERS

University of Illinois at Urbana

Preface

We perceive masculine and feminine roles in the way that St. Paul said we perceive spiritual matters: through a glass, darkly. This is because years of conditioning have caused us to approach almost all situations with male or female preconceptions. We cannot achieve "objectivity" about sexual roles; we can only achieve a degree of understanding at best.

Understanding ourselves is always a difficult task. Most role-oriented discussions focus on the roles of others, and only a careful consideration of a wide range of roles helps us to perceive our own with some clarity. When confronted with certain roles, we experience a feeling that "I am not like that," yet the step is long from such a recognition of what we are not to an awareness of what and who we are. But coming to grips with our own identity is essential: notice the confusion of those who say they have no personal worth or that they feel no kinship for the society of others. Understanding the roles we (as individuals) must play (as human beings) makes us aware of the impact and significance of roles and of what our own roles cumulatively add up to. Exploring our roles and those of others also makes us more aware of what it is to be human. As Father Walter J. Ong suggests, "Acting a role, realizing in a specially intense way one's identity (in a sense) with someone who (in another sense) one is not, remains one of the most human things a man can do."

Our internal world is bound inextricably to the world outside us, and understanding our male or female roles largely determines our ability to deal with organizations and individuals who seek to recreate us in their own images. Many forces try to establish and to manipulate our identities: political groups (left, right, and center) want us to dress and to conduct ourselves in particular ways and to adopt behavior consistent with certain beliefs; advertisers urge us to adopt various roles (as well as to achieve our sexuality) through the use of their products or services (you'll walk with confidence when you wear our shirt; no man can resist you when you wear our pantyhose). Schools and teachers want us to be one thing, parents another, peers another, the draft board another, and so on.

We are caught in the middle of a bewildering cross fire. Too many people want us to be too many things. We understand the need to act differently in various situations, but it is difficult to comprehend how these demands relate to the limited range of roles that make up a single personality. Why are certain things expected only of boys and men, and others only of girls and women? We cannot answer, but we're programmed to respond and we do respond.

Facing the roles that we must (or refuse to) fulfill is a first step in the process of communication. We know certain words must be spoken to parents and others to friends. We know a history teacher does not want the same language in a term paper that men use at a poker party. Most people know that they must alter their language and presentation of themselves when talking or writing to different sorts of people. The young, the middle-aged, the old, those in positions of authority or influence, members of the opposite sex—each must be dealt with in separate terms and styles. Intuitively we know that various types of people have certain expectations about the way we present ourselves, and we alter our responses accordingly—at least we do if we want them to listen to us.

This kind of behavior on our part does not mean we are putting on a front, although that unfortunately happens and is consequently an important aspect of the ethics of communication. Instead, it means that we are at least trying to be sensitive to the feelings and needs of others. Even such common words as "Hi!" "Hello!" "Greetings!" "How the hell are you!" "Good morning!" or "Hey, man!" differ little in literal meaning, but the potential effects on the person spoken to depend greatly on the phrase chosen as well as on the method and style of delivery.

Traditionally, sexual roles are one of the key determinants of how people respond to each other. Boys and men are "supposed to" talk, act, and be treated in one way, girls and women in another. This textbook explores the varieties of sexually defined roles in order to show how some of the ways people define roles affect both themselves and others. To draw on the widest possible range of perceptions and experiences, a variety of genres of communication and of voices is used to demonstrate role perceptions. It would be convenient if a single writer could accurately and objectively articulate all (or even some) aspects of masculinity or femininity. But this is wistful thought because most writers on masculinity or femininity are prompted to write in the first place by strong preoccupations. Some of the most elaborate intellectual arguments on sexuality are only cooked up after the fact to support a particular viewpoint which is emotional in origin.

Consequently a pluralistic and critical approach must be the basic tool of a reader trying to comprehend the materials of those who comment on sexuality. And certainly the senses cannot be left out of this process, since our perceptions of and responses to masculinity and femininity are sensory in origin. In dealing with definitions of masculinity or femininity, or with what some commentators consider the "rightness" or "truth" or "ethics" of socially or biologically determined roles, one must actively involve his entire sensory apparatus as well as his mind. A person's mind can wish away physical manifestations of sexuality; his sensory organs cannot. Neither mind nor senses can receive full trust, nor does either deserve distrust; as in everyday life, they are complements.

As you read the works presented here, you are encouraged to regard the textual materials as springboards to personal experiences and to the variety of sensory and intellectual methods by which masculinity and femininity are perceived in daily life. In written, oral, or visual exercises, try the use of some of the methods by which you ordinarily receive information about masculinity or femininity. After all, most of what you have already learned about being male or female comes from various perceptions of sound, sight, touch, and even smell and taste. By extending the communicative potentials of print with materials at least partially sensory in origin, you will learn more about the processes of communication as well as about masculine and feminine identity.

JOHN HARRINGTON

Contents

Male and Female: Identity

Genesis

So God created man in his own image, in the image of God created he him; male and female created he them. And God blessed them, and God said unto them, "Be fruitful, and multiply, and replenish the earth, and subdue it, and have dominion over the fish of the sea, and over the fowl of the air, and over every living thing that moveth upon the earth."

1.   Distinguish among the various meanings of "man," "men," "woman," and "women." Why is the word "man" used in this passage rather than the word "men"? How do the words "male and female created he them" affect meaning?

2.   What is the "image" of man? Gather representative samples of the image of man from several pictorial sources such as newspapers, magazines, and books with reproductions of classical and modern paintings and sculpture. Recall also the various human images found in literature and film. Are the images of man identical among the various media? Does clothing (or the lack of it) alter the image? Are the various images of man "symbolic," that is, do they move beyond "image" and begin assuming various meanings and implications? Assemble various pictures, samples of poetry, excerpts from literature, and recollections of films into a pictorial–print examination of your concept of the image of man.

And the Lord God planted a garden eastward in Eden; and there he put the man whom he had formed. And out of the ground made the Lord God to grow every tree that is pleasant to the sight and good for food: the tree of life also in the midst of the garden, and the tree of knowledge of good and evil. . . . And the Lord God took the man, and put him into the garden of Eden, to dress it and to keep it. And the Lord God commanded the man, saying, "Of every tree of the garden thou mayest freely eat. But of the tree of the knowledge of good and evil, thou shalt not eat of it: for in the day that thou eatest thereof thou shalt surely die."

And the Lord God said, "It is not good that the man should be alone: I will make him an help meet for him." And out of the ground the Lord God formed every beast of the field, and every fowl of the air, and brought them unto Adam, to see what he would call them: and whatsoever Adam called every living creature, that was the name thereof. And Adam gave names to all cattle, and to the fowl of the air, and to every beast of the field: but for Adam there was not found an help meet for him. And the Lord God caused a deep sleep to fall upon Adam, and he slept: and he took one of his ribs, and closed up the flesh instead thereof. And the rib which the Lord God had taken from man, made he a woman, and brought her unto the man. And Adam said, "This is now bone of my bones, and flesh of my flesh: she shall be called woman, because she was taken out of man." Therefore shall a man leave his father and his mother, and shall cleave unto his wife: and they shall be one flesh. And they were both naked, the man and his wife, and were not ashamed.

Now the serpent was more subtle than any beast of the field which the Lord God had made, and he said unto the woman, "Yea, hath God said, 'Ye shall not eat of every tree of the garden'?" And the woman said unto the serpent, "We may eat of the fruit of the trees of the garden: but of the fruit of the tree which is in the midst of the garden, God hath said, 'Ye shall not eat of it, neither shall ye touch it, lest ye die.'" And the serpent said unto the woman, "Ye shall not surely die. For God doth know that in the day ye eat thereof, then your eyes shall be opened: and ye shall be as gods, knowing good and evil." And when the woman saw that the tree was good for food, and that it was pleasant to the eyes, and a tree to be desired to make one wise, she took of the fruit thereof, and did eat, and gave also unto her husband with her, and he did eat. And the eyes of them both were opened, and they knew that they were naked, and they sewed fig leaves together, and made themselves aprons. And they heard the voice of the Lord God walking in the garden in the cool of the day: and Adam and his wife hid themselves from the presence of the Lord God, amongst the trees of the garden.

And the Lord God called unto Adam, and said unto him, "Where art thou?" And he said, "I heard thy voice in the garden: and I was afraid, because I was naked, and I hid myself." And he said, "Who told thee that thou wast naked? Hast thou eaten of the tree whereof I commanded thee that thou shouldst not eat?" And the man said, "The woman whom thou gavest to be with me, she gave me of the tree, and I did eat." And the Lord God said unto the woman, "What is this that thou hast done?" And the woman said, "The serpent beguiled me, and I did eat." And the Lord God said unto the serpent, "Because thou hast done this, thou art cursed above all cattle, and above every beast of the field: upon thy belly shalt thou go, and dust shalt thou eat, all the days of thy life. And I will put enmity between thee and the woman, and between thy seed and her seed: it shall bruise thy head, and thou shalt bruise his heel." Unto the woman he said, "I will greatly multiply thy sorrow and thy conception. In sorrow thou shalt bring forth children: and thy desire shall be to thy husband, and he shall rule over thee." And unto Adam he said, "Because thou hast hearkened unto the voice of thy wife, and hast eaten of the tree, of which I commanded thee, saying, 'Thou shalt not eat of it': cursed is the ground for thy sake: in sorrow shalt thou eat of it all the days of thy life. Thorns also and thistles shall it bring forth to thee: and thou shalt eat the herb of the field. In the sweat of thy face shalt thou eat bread, till thou return unto the ground: for out of it wast thou taken, for dust thou art, and unto dust shalt thou return." And Adam called his wife's name Eve, because she was the mother of all living. Unto Adam also, and to his wife, did the Lord God make coats of skins, and clothed them.

And the Lord God said, "Behold, the man is become as one of us, to know good and evil. And now, lest he put forth his hand, and take also of the tree of life, and eat and live for ever—": therefore the Lord God sent him forth from the garden of Eden, to till the ground from whence he was taken. So he drove out the man: and he placed at the east of the garden of Eden cherubim, and a flaming sword which turned every way, to keep the way of the tree of life.

Questions

3. Does Eve's creation from Adam's rib define her role as a woman? Would the independent creation of woman alter the meaning and significance of the creation myth? Would it alter the importance for man of Eve's later "betrayal"?

4. Is Adam less guilty than Eve? When he talks to God does Adam blame everything on her?

5. How does God's punishment alter the masculine and feminine roles of Adam and Eve?

6. Does the presentation of male and female roles in Biblical language and mythology affect your response? How?

7. Try telling the story of Adam and Eve in current slang. Do changes in wording affect the meaning or believability of the creation story?

FROM *Songs for Eve*

_____

ARCHIBALD MACLEISH

What Eve Said

Eve said:
From tree to tree
Will journey be;
The one, she said,
Alive and green,
The other dead,
And what's between,
Eve said,.
Our lives mean.

Eve said:
With tree began
That traveller, man;
With tree, she said,
Will journey end.
That tree, though dead,
Its leaves will spend,
Eve said,
World without end.

What Adam Said

My life began
Not when I was moulded man
But when beneath the apple tree
I saw what none but I could see:
Adam flesh and Adam bone
And Adam by himself alone.

That day he sees
His own two hands, those mysteries—
His flesh, his bone and yet not his—
That day man knows himself, and is.

The Fall!

      said Eve;
That Fall began
What leaves conceive
Nor fishes can—
So far a flight
Past touch, past sight.

Collected Poems 1917–1952. Copyright, © 1962 by Archibald MacLeish. Reprinted by permission of the publisher, Houghton Mifflin Company.

Eve said:
The first in his
Whose world this is:
The last, she said,
Blossomed and blown
Though wood be dead,
Is mine, my own.
Eve said:
O my son! O my son!

Get down, said Eve
Upon your shins,
Upon your shanks,
And pray reprieve,
And give God thanks
For Eden sins.

The Fall! she said—
From earth to God!
Give thanks, said she, for branch,
    for bole,
For Eve who found the grace to
    fall
From Adam, browsing animal,
Into the soaring of the soul!

Adam in the Evening

Beauty cannot be shown
But only at remove:
What's beautiful is known
By opposites, as love.

Counter, the mind can see.
When first Eve disobeyed
And turned and looked at me,
Beauty was made.

That distance in the blood
Whereby the eyes have sight
Is love—not understood
But infinite.

Eve in the Dawn

Time created out of clay
That animal with whom I lay.

Like she of wolf or lion's she
In season he would tumble me,

Yet touched me never till he
    took
The apple from my hand and
    Look!

Look! he said, your eyes that see
My eyes have images of me!

That night until the next of day
We touched in love and loving
    lay:

We were awake then who had
    slept.
Our bodies out of Eden leapt

Together to a lifted place
Past space of time and time of
    space

That neither space nor time had
    made.

There first we laughed, were
    first afraid.

Was it Adam, only he,
Bred that flowering branch of
    me
Whereon shall hang eternity?

Questions

1. Examine the personae (the dramatic personalities of the
speakers) emerging from these poems. Do you detect differences
in concerns, attitudes toward self, or thoughts about the significance
of the fall?

2. Do these poems restate the Biblical account, or do they
modify it?

3. Was the fall harmful or beneficial to men and women?
What are the values you bring to a personal answer of this
question (or to a rejection of its validity)?

4. Why do you suppose the story of Adam and Eve has in-
trigued so many people for thousands of years? In what ways
is the story "true"?

5. Since the story of Adam and Eve is questionable on a literal
level and cannot be proved with any of the methods of modern
science, would children be better off hearing only scientific explanations of the creation?

6. What are the dominant images normally connected with the
story of Adam and Eve? Does the language of *Genesis* and of
MacLeish add to these images? What aspects of the fall can be
communicated most effectively through language? Through
pictures? Through film? Through sound?

Samson and Delilah

And it came to pass afterward, that [Samson] loved a woman in the valley of Sorek, whose name was Delilah. And the lords of the Philistines came up unto her, and said unto her, "Entice him, and see wherein his great strength lieth, and by what means we may prevail against him, that we may bind him, to afflict him: and we will give thee every one of us eleven hundred pieces of silver."

And Delilah said to Samson, "Tell me, I pray thee, wherein thy great strength lieth, and wherewith thou mightest be bound, to afflict thee." And Samson said unto her, "If they bind me with seven green withes that were never dried, then shall I be weak, and be as another man." Then the lords of the Philistines brought up to her seven green withes which had not been dried, and she bound him with them. Now there were men lying in wait, abiding with her in the chamber: and she said unto him, "The Philistines be upon thee, Samson." And he brake the withes, as a thread of tow is broken when it toucheth the fire: so his strength was not known. And Delilah said unto Samson, "Behold, thou hast mocked me, and told me lies: now tell me, I pray thee, wherewith thou mightest be bound." And he said unto her, "If they bind me fast with new ropes that never were occupied, then shall I be weak, and be as another man." Delilah therefore took new ropes, and bound him therewith, and said unto him, "The Philistines be upon thee, Samson." (And there were liers in wait abiding in the chamber.) And he brake them from off his arms, like a thread. And Delilah said unto Samson, "Hitherto thou hast mocked me, and told me lies: tell me wherewith thou mightest be bound." And he said unto her, "If thou weavest the seven locks of my head with the web." And she fastened it with the pin, and said unto him, "The Philistines be upon thee, Samson." And he awaked out of his sleep, and went away with the pin of the beam, and with the web.

And she said unto him, "How canst thou say, 'I love thee,' when thine heart is not with me? Thou hast mocked me these three times, and hast not told me wherein thy great strength lieth." And it came to pass, when she pressed him daily with her words, and urged him, so that his soul was vexed unto death, that he told her all his heart, and said unto her, "There hath not come a razor upon mine head: for I have been a Nazarite unto God from my mother's womb: if I be shaven, then my strength will go from me, and I shall become weak, and be like any other man." And when Delilah saw that he had told her all his heart, she sent and called for the lords of the Philistines, saying, "Come up this once, for he hath showed me all his heart." Then the lords of the Philistines came up unto her, and brought money in their hand. And she made him sleep upon her knees, and she called for a man, and she caused him to shave off the seven locks of his head, and she began to afflict him, and his strength went from him. And she said, "The Philistines be upon thee, Samson." And he awoke out of his sleep, and said, "I will go out as at other times before, and shake myself." And he wist not that the Lord was departed from him.

But the Philistines took him, and put out his eyes, and brought him down to Gaza, and bound him with fetters of brass, and he did grind in the prison house. Howbeit the hair of his head began to grow again, after he was shaven. Then the lords of the Philistines gathered them together, for to offer a great sacrifice unto Dagon their god, and to rejoice: for they said, "Our god hath delivered Samson our enemy into our hand." And when the people saw him, they praised their god: for they said, "Our god hath delivered into our hands our enemy, and the destroyer of our country, which slew many of us." And it came to pass when their hearts were merry, that they said, "Call for Samson, that he may make us sport." And they called for Samson out of the prison house, and he made them sport, and they set him between the pillars. And Samson said unto the lad that held him by the hand, "Suffer me, that I may feel the pillars whereupon the house standeth, that I may lean upon them."

Now the house was full of men and women, and all the lords of the Philistines were there: and there were upon the roof about three thousand men and women, that beheld while Samson made sport. And Samson called unto the Lord, and said, "O Lord God, remember me, I pray thee, and strengthen me, I pray thee, only this once, O God, that I may be at once avenged of the Philistines, for my two eyes." And Samson took hold of the two middle pillars, upon which the house stood, and on which it was borne up, of the one with his right hand, and of the other with his left. And Samson said, "Let me die with the Philistines": and he bowed himself with all his might: and the house fell upon the lords, and upon all the people that were therein. So the dead which he slew at his death were more than they which he slew in his life.

Questions

1.   Delilah is the second woman the Philistines use in their attempt to discover the secret of Samson's strength. Why do you think a woman is used to bring about Samson's downfall?

2.   What differences do you detect between Samson's male "cunning" and Delilah's female "wiles"?

3.   Is Samson's suicide an assertion of his masculinity?

4.   How is the Biblical view of masculinity and femininity like and unlike the twentieth-century American view(s) of sexually defined roles?

5.   Hair, a symbol of strength in this story, traditionally has been associated with masculinity. Does our culture regard hair as a symbol of masculinity? Have recent hair styles had any effect on the way we respond to hair?

Hair

GEROME RAGNI AND JAMES RADO

SHE ASKS ME WHY . . .

I'M JUST A HAIRY GUY
I'M HAIRY NOON AND NIGHT
HAIR THAT'S A FRIGHT

I'M HAIRY HIGH AND LOW
DON'T ASK ME WHY—DON'T KNOW

IT'S NOT FOR LACK OF BREAD
LIKE THE GRATEFUL DEAD

DARLIN'
GIVE ME A HEAD WITH HAIR
LONG BEAUTIFUL HAIR
SHINING GLEAMING STREAMING
FLAXEN WAXEN

GIVE ME DOWN TO THERE HAIR
SHOULDER-LENGTH OR LONGER
AS LONG AS GOD CAN GROW IT

FLOW IT
SHOW IT

HAIR HAIR
HAIR HAIR HAIR
HAIR HAIR HAIR

FLOW IT
SHOW IT
LONG AS GOD CAN GROW IT
MY HAIR

LET IT FLY IN THE BREEZE
AND GET CAUGHT IN THE TREES
GIVE A HOME TO THE FLEAS
IN MY HAIR

A HOME FOR FLEAS
A HIVE FOR BEES
A NEST FOR BIRDS
THERE AINT NO WORDS
FOR THE BEAUTY THE SPLENDOR
THE WONDER OF MY

HAIR HAIR
HAIR HAIR HAIR
HAIR HAIR HAIR

FLOW IT
SHOW IT
LONG AS GOD CAN GROW IT
MY HAIR

I WANT IT LONG STRAIGHT CURLY
        FUZZY
SNAGGY SHAGGY RATTY MATTY
OILY GREASY FLEECY
SHINING GLEAMING STREAMING
FLAXEN WAXEN
KNOTTED POLKADOTTED
TWISTED BEADED BRAIDED
POWDERED FLOWERED AND
        CONFETTIED
BANGLED TANGLED SPANGLED AND
        SPAGHETTIED

OH SAY CAN YOU SEE MY EYES
IF YOU CAN
THEN MY HAIR'S TOO SHORT

DOWN TO HERE
DOWN TO THERE
DOWN TO WHERE
IT STOPS BY ITSELF

DOO DOO DOO DOO DOO DOO DOO DOO
    DOO DOO
DOO DOO DOO DOO DOO DOO DOO DOO
    DOO DOO

THEY'LL BE GA GA AT THE GO GO
WHEN THEY SEE ME IN MY TOGA
MY TOGA MADE OF BLOND
    BRILLIANTINED
BIBLICAL HAIR

MY HAIR LIKE JESUS WORE IT
HALLELUJAH I ADORE IT

HALLELUJAH MARY LOVED HER SON
WHY DON'T MOTHER LOVE ME

HAIR HAIR
HAIR HAIR HAIR
HAIR HAIR HAIR

FLOW IT
SHOW IT
LONG AS GOD CAN GROW IT
MY HAIR

Male and Female: Identity

Rulko/D.P.I.

Cornell Capa/Magnum
Paul Thomas/Black Star

Joe Covello/Black Star

My Conviction

GEROME RAGNI AND JAMES RADO

I WOULD JUST LIKE TO SAY THAT IT IS
    MY CONVICTION
THAT LONGER HAIR AND OTHER
    FLAMBOYANT AFFECTATIONS
OF APPEARANCE ARE NOTHING MORE
THAN THE MALE'S EMERGENCE FROM
    HIS DRAB CAMOUFLAGE

INTO THE GAUDY PLUMAGE
WHICH IS THE BIRTHRIGHT OF HIS SEX

THERE IS A PECULIAR NOTION THAT
    ELEGANT PLUMAGE
AND FINE FEATHERS ARE NOT PROPER
    FOR THE MAN
WHEN ACTUALLY THAT IS THE WAY
    THINGS ARE
IN MOST SPECIES

Questions

1.   What sort of masculinity do the songs *Hair* and *My Conviction* advocate? What sort of femininity?

2.   In what ways is hair a symbol?

3.   Is it easier to accept the ideas of these songs because they are dramatically set to music?

4.   How would different segments of the American people respond to the vision of masculinity and femininity found in these songs?

5.   Do *Hair* and *My Conviction* "sound" masculine? What are the sounds associated with masculinity in our culture? Try recording various sounds that are acceptable and encouraged among boys and men, then try the same thing with sounds associated with girls and women. Can these sounds be assembled to make a statement supporting or attacking a particular view of masculinity or femininity?

Ballad of Willie Joe Namath

VERNON SCOTT

Once upon a time on the planet Earth in ancient 20th Century America there thrived the last of a tribe known as gladiators.

They were not warriors who marched to drums.

Highly Valued

Rather, they were like certain Romans who preceded them by several hundred years.

Romans dubbed their fiercest fighters gladiators. They competed in games of great brutality to the glee of the populace. Americans refined the term to football player.

The populace valued these gladiators more highly than warriors, statesmen, scientists and philosophers. They were showered with gold, and often sat at the right hand of politicians.

Most uncommon of the American gladiators was man known as Willie Joe Namath who could hurl a ball more accurately than the Romans wielded trident or spear.

He was courageous for his legs were hobbled. He could not run. He lived as a prince in rich surroundings, women on all sides, and was hailed a hero wherever he traveled.

Reprinted by permission of Vernon Scott and United Press International.

NBC Photo   Travis Sehman/Globe Photos

Willie Joe was not a savage, but he faced 280-pound giants bent on disassociating his head from his shoulders.

In Motion Pictures

Namath was a quarterback—the definition of which is lost in antiquity. But he also became a minstrel (or actor) in three motion pictures (a 20th Century art form): "Norwood," "C.C. and Company" and "The Last Rebel."

He also partook of a television (another ancient craft) show titled "The Super Comedy Bowl" which records indicate was beamed Jan. 10, 1971 and included mummers of the day and other gladiators.

A United Press International dispatch of that era survives, preserving some of Willie Joe Namath's thoughts on his brutal way of life.

"Football has been my way of life," he said. "I feel more comfortable on the field than I do acting. Everybody on both teams went through the same thing to become pros."

Namath indicated football players, like gladiators before them, were especially trained to receive and administer punishment.

Much of Namath's nomenclature of Barbary is lost in the mists of history. But one cannot doubt his courage.

"I'm used to having men twice my size try to put me face," Namath said. "I've had them try to twist my head off when I'm knocked down in a pile-up.

"But when you are part of something you cherish, something that has given you everything in life—like football you do what you can to help it.

"I would never say or write anything detrimental about football. I have been injured. But that is part of the game. You accept it.

"Anyway," Namath said, "Winning solves all the problems."

Questions

1. Why do you think the author assumes the role of a writer observing Earth from some distant point in time? Does such a stance improve or detract from his credibility as a commentator?

2. How does the apparently large time perspective of the writer affect his comparison of football players with gladiators? Why does Scott define the actions of gladiators?

3. Why do you think the writer focuses on Namath?

4. In what way is football "masculine"? Can you think of objections to some aspect of football's "male mystique"? Does football contribute anything to society?

5. From the point of view of a twenty-fifth-century historian, write a short essay on the ways advertisers of the twentieth century associated particular products (such as cigarettes, cars, deodorants, or lipsticks) with masculinity and femininity.

To Lucasta, Going to the Wars

—————————————————

RICHARD LOVELACE

Tell me not, sweet, I am unkind,
    That from the nunnery
Of thy chaste breast and quiet mind
    To war and arms I fly.

True, a new mistress now I chase,
    The first foe in the field;
And with a stronger faith embrace
    A sword, a horse, a shield.

Yet this inconstancy is such
    As you too shall adore;
I could not love thee, dear, so much,
    Loved I not honor more.

Questions

1.   Does the creed voiced by Lovelace still exist today? If so, where do we see it expressed? Does the relationship among "honor," "war," and "love" affect our lives in the twentieth century?

2.   Write a poem to someone explaining why "honor" (what modern words are appropriate here?) causes you to do something against the wishes of the person addressed or a poem objecting to something the addressee feels compelled by "honor" to do.

3.   Use Lovelace's poem as the basis for a collage made from contemporary magazine photographs. You may either convey the poem's ideas in pictures or use visual images to directly contradict what the poem tries to say.

My First Goose

ISAAC BABEL

Savitsky, Commander of the VI Division, rose when he saw me, and I wondered at the beauty of his giant's body. He rose, the purple of his riding breeches and the crimson of his little tilted cap and the decorations stuck on his chest cleaving the hut as a standard cleaves the sky. A smell of scent and the sickly sweet freshness of soap emanated from him. His long legs were like girls sheathed to the neck in shining riding boots.

He smiled at me, struck his riding whip on the table, and drew toward him an order that the Chief of Staff had just finished dictating. It was an order for Ivan Chesnokov to advance on Chugunov-Dobry-vodka with the regiment entrusted to him, to make contact with the enemy and destroy the same.

"For which destruction," the Commander began to write, smearing the whole sheet, "I make this same Chesnokov entirely responsible, up to and including the supreme penalty, and will if necessary strike him down on the spot; which you, Chesnokov, who have been working with me at the front for some months now, cannot doubt."

The Commander signed the order with a flourish, tossed it to his orderlies and turned upon me gray eyes that danced with merriment.

Reprinted by permission of S. G. Phillips, Inc. from *The Collected Stories of Isaac Babel*. Copyright © 1955 by S. G. Phillips, Inc.

I handed him a paper with my appointment to the Staff of the Division.

"Put it down in the Order of the Day," said the Commander. "Put him down for every satisfaction save the front one. Can you read and write?"

"Yes, I can read and write," I replied, envying the flower and iron of that youthfulness. "I graduated in law from St. Petersburg University."

"Oh, are you one of those grinds?" he laughed. "Specs on your nose, too! What a nasty little object! They've sent you along without making any enquiries; and this is a hot place for specs. Think you'll get on with us?"

"I'll get on all right," I answered, and went off to the village with the quartermaster to find a billet for the night.

The quartermaster carried my trunk on his shoulder. Before us stretched the village street. The dying sun, round and yellow as a pumpkin, was giving up its roseate ghost to the skies.

We went up to a hut painted over with garlands. The quartermaster stopped, and said suddenly, with a guilty smile:

"Nuisance with specs. Can't do anything to stop it, either. Not a life for the brainy type here. But you go and mess up a lady, and a good lady too, and you'll have the boys patting you on the back."

He hestitated, my little trunk on his shoulder; then he came quite close to me, only to dart away again despairingly and run to the nearest yard. Cossacks were sitting there, shaving one another.

"Here, you soldiers," said the quartermaster, setting my little trunk down on the ground. "Comrade Savitsky's orders are that you're to take this chap in your billets, so no nonsense about it, because the chap's been through a lot in the learning line."

The quartermaster, purple in the face, left us without looking back. I raised my hand to my cap and saluted the Cossacks. A lad with long straight flaxen hair and the handsome face of the Ryazan Cossacks went over to my little trunk and tossed it out at the gate. Then he turned his back on me and with remarkable skill emitted a series of shameful noises.

"To your guns—number double-zero!" an older Cossack shouted at him, and burst out laughing. "Running fire!"

His guileless art exhausted, the lad made off. Then, crawling over the ground, I began to gather together the manuscripts and tattered garments that had fallen out of the trunk. I gathered them up and carried them to the other end of the yard. Near the hut, on a brick stove, stood a cauldron in which pork was cooking. The steam that rose from it was like the far-off smoke of home in the village, and it mingled hunger with desperate loneliness in my head. Then I covered my little broken trunk with hay, turning it into a pillow, and lay down on the ground to read in *Pravda* Lenin's speech at the Second Congress of the Comintern. The sun fell upon me from behind the toothed hillocks, the Cossacks trod on my feet, the lad made fun of me untiringly, the beloved lines came toward me along a thorny path and could not reach me. Then I put aside the paper and went out to the landlady, who was spinning on the porch.

"Landlady," I said, "I've got to eat."

The old woman raised to me the diffused whites of her purblind eyes and lowered them again.

"Comrade," she said, after a pause, "what with all this going on, I want to go and hang myself."

"Christ!" I muttered, and pushed the old woman in the chest with my fist. "You don't suppose I'm going to go into explanations with you, do you?"

And turning around I saw somebody's sword lying within reach. A severe-looking goose was waddling about the yard, inoffensively preening its feathers. I overtook it and pressed it to the ground. Its head cracked beneath my boot, cracked and emptied itself. The white neck lay stretched out in the dung, the wings twitched.

"Christ!" I said, digging into the goose with my sword. "Go and cook it for me, landlady."

Her blind eyes and glasses glistening, the old woman picked up the slaughtered bird, wrapped it in her apron, and started to bear it off toward the kitchen.

"Comrade," she said to me, after a while, "I want to go and hang myself." And she closed the door behind her.

The Cossacks in the yard were already sitting around their cauldron. They sat motionless, stiff as heathen priests at a sacrifice, and had not looked at the goose.

"The lad's all right," one of them said, winking and scooping up the cabbage soup with his spoon.

The Cossacks commenced their supper with all the elegance and restraint of peasants who respect one another. And I wiped the sword with sand, went out at the gate, and came in again, depressed. Already the moon hung above the yard like a cheap earring.

"Hey, you," suddenly said Surovkov, an older Cossack. "Sit down and feed with us till your goose is done."

He produced a spare spoon from his boot and handed it to me. We supped up the cabbage soup they had made, and ate the pork.

"What's in the newspaper?" asked the flaxen-haired lad, making room for me.

"Lenin writes in the paper," I said, pulling out *Pravda*. "Lenin writes that there's a shortage of everything."

And loudly, like a triumphant man hard of hearing, I read Lenin's speech out to the Cossacks.

Evening wrapped about me the quickening moisture of its twilight sheets; evening laid a mother's hand upon my burning forehead. I read on and rejoiced, spying out exultingly the secret curve of Lenin's straight line.

"Truth tickles everyone's nostrils," said Surovkov, when I had come to the end. "The question is, how's it to be pulled from the heap. But he goes and strikes at it straight off like a hen pecking at a grain!"

This remark about Lenin was made by Surovkov, platoon commander of the Staff Squadron; after which we lay down to sleep in the hayloft. We slept, all six of us, beneath a wooden roof that let in the stars, warming one another, our legs intermingled. I dreamed: and in my dreams saw women. But my heart, stained with bloodshed, grated and brimmed over.

Questions

1. Why is the young man finally accepted by the Cossacks? Why does his heart grate and brim over after he is accepted? What changes occur in his behavior during the story?

2. What are some of the initiation rituals a boy in our culture must undergo to be recognized as a man? What rituals must girls undergo?

3. How would a social scientist treat the problem Isaac Bable deals with in this story? What advantages does the format of a story offer? What disadvantages?

4. What are the "signs" of masculinity and femininity that older people in our society look for in boys and girls? What "signs" do members of the peer group look for?

5. From your personal experience, select an incident which you think was part of your initiation into manhood or womanhood. Try writing about this incident in story form, showing the painfulness of the situation and how you responded.

Lament

D Y L A N   T H O M A S

When I was a windy boy and a bit
And the black spit of the chapel fold,
(Sighed the old ram rod, dying of women),
I tiptoed shy in the gooseberry wood,
The rude owl cried like a telltale tit,
I skipped in a blush as the big girls rolled
Ninepin down on the donkeys' common,
And on seesaw sunday nights I wooed
Whoever I would with my wicked eyes,   `
The whole of the moon I could love and leave
All the green leaved little weddings' wives
In the coal black bush and let them grieve.

When I was a gusty man and a half
And the black beast of the beetles' pews,
(Sighed the old ram rod, dying of bitches),
Not a boy and a bit in the wick-
Dipping moon and drunk as a new dropped calf,
I whistled all night in the twisted flues,
Midwives grew in the midnight ditches,
And the sizzling beds of the town cried, Quick!—

Whenever I dove in a breast high shoal,
Wherever I ramped in the clover quilts,
Whatsoever I did in the coal-
Black night, I left my quivering prints.

When I was a man you could call a man
And the black cross of the holy house,
(Sighed the old ram rod, dying of welcome),
Brandy and ripe in my bright, bass prime,
No springtailed tom in the red hot town
With every simmering woman his mouse
But a hillocky bull in the swelter
Of summer come in his great good time
To the sultry, biding herds, I said,
Oh, time enough when the blood creeps cold,
And I lie down but to sleep in bed,
For my sulking, skulking, coal black soul!

When I was a half of the man I was
And serve me right as the preachers warn,
(Sighed the old ram rod, dying of downfall),
No flailing calf or cat in a flame
Or hickory bull in milky grass
But a black sheep with a crumpled horn,
At last the soul from its foul mousehole
Slung pouting out when the limp time came;
And I gave my soul a blind, slashed eye,
Gristle and rind, and a roarers' life,
And I shoved it into the coal black sky
To find a woman's soul for a wife.

Now I am a man no more no more
And a black reward for a roaring life,
(Sighed the old ram rod, dying of strangers),
Tidy and cursed in my dove cooed room
I lie down thin and hear the good bells jaw—
For, oh, my soul found a sunday wife
In the coal black sky and she bore angels!
Harpies around me out of her womb!
Chastity prays for me, piety sings,
Innocence sweetens my last black breath,
Modesty hides my thighs in her wings,
And all the deadly virtues plague my death!

Questions

1. Listen to Dylan Thomas' reading of "Lament" (available on Caedmon Records). What changes do you detect in his voice? How are these changes geared to the changing life of the poem's speaker?

2. Construct a prose or poetic monologue in which some change can be noticed in the speaker's attitude toward a subject although he never actually tells you explicitly what the change is.

The Flea

JOHN DONNE

Marke but this flea, and marke in this,
How little that which thou deny'st me is;
It suck'd me first, and now sucks thee,
And in this flea, our two bloods mingled bee;
Thou know'st that this cannot be said
A sinne, nor shame, nor losse of maidenhead,
　　Yet this enjoyes before it wooe,
　　And pamper'd swells with one blood made of two,
　　And this, alas, is more then wee would doe.

Oh stay, three lives in one flea spare,
Where wee almost, yea more then maryed are.
This flea is you and I, and this
Our mariage bed, and mariage temple is;
Though parents grudge, and you, w'are met,
And cloysterd in these living walls of Jet.
　　Though use make you apt to kill mee,
　　Let not to that, selfe murder added bee,
　　And sacrilege, three sinnes in killing three.

Cruell and sodaine, hast thou since
Purpled thy naile, in blood of innocence?
Wherein could this flea guilty bee,

Except in that drop which it suckt from thee?
Yet thou triumph'st, and saist that thou
Find'st not thy selfe, nor mee the weaker now;
　　'Tis true, then learne how false, feares bee;
　　Just so much honor, when thou yeeld'st to mee,
　　Will wast, as this flea's death tooke life from thee.

Questions

1. Is the speaker's seduction argument a good one? Would it be likely to convince most girls? The speaker obviously hopes his words will result in success, but does the poet agree with the speaker's line of argument? Or is John Donne showing us the speaker in such a way that what the latter says will appear ironic? Does the speaker grasp the implications of the religious allusions found in his words? Are these allusions important to the poem's meaning?

2. Try writing a short poem or prose monologue in which you present a speaker who takes himself quite seriously but whom you want the reader to see as foolish. For example, you might depict a general talking about the joys of war or a high school principal explaining how this generation of students has "gone to the dogs."

Playboy's Doctrine of Male

HARVEY COX

Sometime this month over one million American young men will place sixty cents on a counter somewhere and walk away with a copy of *Playboy,* one of the most spectacular successes in the entire history of American journalism. When one remembers that every copy will probably be seen by several other people in college dormitories and suburban rumpus rooms, the total readership in any one month easily exceeds that of all the independent religious magazines, serious political and cultural journals, and literary periodicals put together.

What accounts for this uncanny reception? What factors in American life have combined to allow *Playboy's* ambitious young publisher, Hugh Hefner, to pyramid his jackpot into a chain of night clubs, TV spectaculars, bachelor tours to Europe and special discount cards? What impact does *Playboy* really have?

Clearly *Playboy's* astonishing popularity is not attributable solely to pin-up girls. For sheer nudity its pictorial art cannot compete with such would-be competitors as *Dude* and *Escapade.* Rather, *Playboy* appeals to a highly mobile, increasingly affluent group of young readers, mostly between eighteen and thirty, who want much more from

Reprinted from the April 17, 1971 issue of *Christianity and Crisis,* permission granted by Christianity and Crisis, Inc.

their drugstore reading than bosoms and thighs. They need a total image of what it means to be a man. And Mr. Hefner's *Playboy* has no hesitancy about telling them.

Why should such a need arise? David Riesman has argued that the responsibility for character formation in our society has shifted from the family to the peer group and to the mass media peer group surrogates. Things are changing so rapidly that one who is equipped by his family with inflexible, highly internalized values becomes unable to deal with the accelerated pace of change and with the varying contexts in which he is called upon to function. This is especially true in the area of consumer values toward which the "other-directed person" is increasingly oriented.

Within the confusing plethora of mass media signals and peer group values, *Playboy* fills a special need. For the insecure young man with newly acquired time and money on his hands who still feels uncertain about his consumer skills, *Playboy* supplies a comprehensive and authoritative guidebook to this foreboding new world to which he now has access. It tells him not only who to be; it tells him *how* to be it, and even provides consolation outlets for those who secretly feel that they have not quite made it.

In supplying for the other-directed consumer of leisure both the normative identity image and the means for achieving it, *Playboy* relies on a careful integration of copy and advertising material. The comic book that appeals to a younger generation with an analogous problem skillfully intersperses illustrations of incredibly muscled men and excessively mammalian women with advertisements for body-building gimmicks and foam rubber brassiere supplements. Thus the thin-chested comic book readers of both sexes are thoughtfully supplied with both the ends and the means for attaining a spurious brand of maturity. *Playboy* merely continues the comic book tactic for the next age group. Since within every identity crisis, whether in 'teens or twenties, there is usually a sexual identity problem, *Playboy* speaks to those who desperately want to know what it means to be a *man,* and more specifically a *male,* in today's world.

Both the image of man and the means for its attainment exhibit a remarkable consistency in *Playboy*. The skilled consumer is cool and unruffled. He savors sports cars, liquor, high fidelity and book club selections with a casual, unhurried aplomb. Through he must certainly *have* and *use* the latest consumption item, he must not permit himself to get too attached to it. The style will change and he must always be ready to adjust. His persistent anxiety that he may mix a drink incorrectly, enjoy a jazz group that is passé, or wear last year's necktie style is comforted by an authoritative tone in *Playboy* beside which papal encyclicals sound irresolute.

"Don't hesitate," he is told, "this assertive, self-assured weskit is what every man of taste wants for the fall season." Lingering doubts about his masculinity are extirpated by the firm assurance that "real men demand this ruggedly masculine smoke" (cigar ad). Though "the ladies will swoon for you, no matter what they promise, don't give them a puff. This cigar is for men only." A fur-lined canvas field jacket is described as "the most masculine thing since the cave man." What to be and how to be it are both made unambiguously clear.

But since being a male necessitates some kind of relationship to females, *Playboy* fearlessly confronts this problem too, and solves it by the consistent application of the same formula. Sex becomes one of the items of leisure activity that the knowledgeable consumer of leisure handles with his characteristic skill and detachment. The girl becomes a desirable, indeed an indispensable "Playboy accessory."

In a question-answering column entitled: "The Playboy Advisor," queries about smoking equipment (how to break in a meerschaum pipe), cocktail preparation (how to mix a "Yellow Fever") and whether or not to wear suspenders with a vest, alternate with questions about what to do with girls who complicate the cardinal principle of casualness, either by suggesting marriage or by some other impulsive gesture toward permanent relationship. The infallible answer from the oracle never varies: sex must be contained, at all costs, within the entertainment-recreation area. Don't let her get "serious."

After all, the most famous feature of the magazine is its monthly fold-out photo of a *play*mate. She is the symbol par excellence of recreational sex. When play time is over, the playmate's function ceases, so she must be made to understand the rules of the game. As the crew-cut young man in a *Playboy* cartoon says to the rumpled and disarrayed girl he is passionately embracing, "Why speak of love at a time like this?"

The magazine's fiction purveys the same kind of severely departmentalized sex. Although the editors have recently dressed up the contents of *Playboy* with contributions by Hemingway, Bemelmans and even a Chekhov translation, the regular run of stories relies on a repetitive and predictable formula. A successful young man, either single or somewhat less than ideally married—a figure with whom readers have no difficulty identifying—encounters a gorgeous and seductive woman who makes no demands on him except sex. She is the prose duplication of the cool-eyed but hot-blooded playmate of the fold-out page.

Drawing heavily on the phantasy life of all young Americans, the writers utilize for their stereotyped heroines the hero's school teacher, his secretary, an old girl friend, or the girl who brings her car into the garage where he works. The happy issue is always a casual but satisfying sexual experience with no entangling alliances whatever. Unlike the women he knows in real life, the *Playboy* reader's fictional girl friends know their place and ask for nothing more. They present no danger of permanent involvement. Like any good accessory, they are detachable and disposable.

Many of the advertisements reinforce the sex-accessory identification in another way by attributing female characteristics to the items they sell. Thus a full page ad for the MG assures us that this car is not only "the smoothest pleasure machine" on the road and that having one is a "love-affair," but most importantly, "you drive it—it doesn't drive you." The ad ends with the equivocal question, "Is it a date?"

Playboy insists that its message is one of liberation. Its gospel frees us from captivity to the puritanical "hat-pin brigade." It solemnly crusades for "frankness" and publishes scores of letters congratulating it for its unblushing "candor." Yet the whole phenomenon of which *Playboy* is only a part vividly illustrates the awful fact of a new kind of tyranny.

Those liberated by technology and increased prosperity to new worlds of leisure now become the anxious slaves of dictatorial tastemakers. Obsequiously waiting for the latest signal on what is cool and what is awkward, they are paralyzed by the fear that they may hear pronounced on them that dread sentence occasionally intoned by "The Playboy Advisor": "you goofed!" Leisure is thus swallowed up in apprehensive competitiveness, its liberating potential transformed into a self-destructive compulsion to consume only what is *au courant*. *Playboy* mediates the Word of the most high into one section of the consumer world, but it is a word of bondage, not of freedom.

Nor will *Playboy's* synthetic doctrine of man stand the test of scrutiny. Psychoanalysts constantly remind us how deeply seated sexuality is in the human self. But if they didn't remind us, we would soon discover it anyway in our own experience. As much as the human male might like to terminate his relationship with a woman as he snaps off the stereo, or store her for special purposes like a camel's hair jacket, it really can't be done. And anyone with a modicum of experience with women knows it can't be done. Perhaps this is the reason why *Playboy's* readership drops off so sharply after the age of thirty.

Playboy really feeds on the presence of a repressed fear of involvement with women, which for various reasons is still present in many otherwise adult Americans. So *Playboy's* version of sexuality grows increasingly irrelevant as authentic sexual maturity is achieved.

The male identity crisis to which *Playboy* speaks has as its roots a deep-set fear of sex, a fear that is uncomfortably combined with fascination. *Playboy* strives to resolve this antinomy by reducing the terrible proportions of sexuality, its power and its passion, to a packageable consumption item. Thus in *Playboy's* iconography, the nude woman symbolizes total sexual accessibility, but demands nothing from the observer. "You drive it—it doesn't drive you." The terror of sex, which cannot be separated from its ecstasy, is dissolved. But this futile attempt to reduce the *mysterium tremendum* of the sexual fails to solve the problem of being a man. For sexuality is the basic form of all human relationship, and therein lies its terror and its power.

Karl Barth has called this basic relational form of man's life *Mitmensch,* co-humanity. This means that becoming fully human, in this case a human male, necessitates not having the other totally exposed to me and my purposes—while I remain uncommitted—but exposing myself to the risk of encounter with the other by reciprocal self-exposure. The story of man's refusal to be so exposed goes back to the story of Eden and is expressed by man's desire to control the other rather than to *be with* the other. It is basically the fear to be one's self, a lack of the "courage to be."

Thus any theological critique of *Playboy* that focuses on its "lewdness" will misfire completely. *Playboy* and its less successful imitators are not "sex magazines" at all. They are basically anti-sexual. They dilute and dissipate authentic sexuality by reducing it to an accessory, by keeping it at a safe distance.

It is precisely because these magazines are anti-sexual that they deserve the most searching kind of theological criticism. They foster a heretical doctrine of man, one at radical variance with the biblical view. For *Playboy's* man, others—especially women—are *for* him. They are his leisure accessories, his playthings. For the Bible, man only becomes fully man by being *for* the other.

Moralistic criticisms of *Playboy* fail because its anti-moralism is one of the few places in which *Playboy* is right. But if Christians bear the name of One who was truly man because he was totally *for* the other, and if it is in him that we know who God is and what human life is for, then we must see in *Playboy* the latest and slickest episode in man's continuing refusal to be fully human.

Questions

1. Does your own reading of *Playboy* confirm Cox's ideas? What evidence of a *Playboy* "identity" do you see around you? Do you see any ways in which *Playboy* is designed to appeal to an audience of college students?

2. In what ways is fantasy healthy? Unhealthy?

3. How can *Playboy* be called antisexual when it deals so extensively with sex?

4. Is Cox's appeal primarily emotional or intellectual? What sort of audience does he have in mind?

5. In "The Cosmo Girl: A Playboy Inversion" (*Christian Advocate*, January 12, 1967), Allen J. Moore asserts that *Cosmopolitan* reads like a female version of *Playboy* and that the "Cosmo Girl" looks very much like the playmate of the playboy's fantasy. The major difference, he finds, is that the Cosmo Girl plays for keeps: "Marriage is her goal!" The Cosmo Girl sees man as an object, an accessory, she can use to obtain guaranteed security. From your own reading of women's magazines (especially *Cosmopolitan*), does such an accusation seem plausible? Surprising?

6. One of the ads always appearing in *Playboy* is based on the theme "What sort of man reads *Playboy?*" Satirize either *Playboy* or *Cosmopolitan* by taking a single copy of either magazine and cutting words, sentences, and pictures from the magazine and arranging them in such a way that you are making fun of or criticizing either some aspect of the magazine or of the publication's supposed view of its reader. For ironic juxtaposition you might want to use pictures and other materials from various magazines which show people very different from those seen in the ads and features of *Playboy* or *Cosmopolitan*. By using visual language, you will be making some comment on your views of a particular publication.

How the American Boy is Feminized

PATRICIA SEXTON

Murders are usually committed by quiet and gentle men, "nice guys." Sirhan and Oswald, both reared under the maternal shadow, grew to be quiet, controlled men and dutiful sons. Estranged from their fellows, fathers, and normal male associations, they joined a rapidly growing breed—the "feminized male"—whose normal male impulses are suppressed or misshapen by overexposure to feminine norms. Other forms of violence that puzzle us—riots, rebellions, revolts— are in large part expressions of suppressed manhood.

The active rebels, as well as the passive hippie protesters, are often middle-class boys, feminized by schools, dominant mothers, and controls that keep them in swaddling clothes. Their desire to get out is simply the natural male impulse to cut maternal ties and become a man. The black revolt is a quest by the black male for power, status and manhood. The black does not want to be a "boy" any longer; *I am a man* is the slogan of his revolt. These rebellions are alarms, alerting us to social forces that dangerously diminish manhood and spread alienation and violence.

It is difficult for societies to deal with the male's aggressive quest for manhood. Since males seem generally unwilling to settle for less without a struggle, they tend to become social "misfits" much more often than women do.

Reprinted by permission of author.

Male suicides greatly outnumber female. About 70 per cent of successful suicides are male. In mental institutions for children, boys outnumber girls three to one. If boys are not more disturbed than girls, they are at least more disturbing, and thus more likely to be hospitalized or otherwise sent away for troubled behavior.

In one urban community, single men were found most likely to be mentally ill, followed, in order, by married women, single women, and married men. The single man is most likely to be an outsider—vagrant, alcoholic, criminal, homosexual, rebel, lunatic.

Other forms of disturbed behavior are also far more common among boys. Boy delinquents outnumber girls about five to one. Gangs of boys are about 300 times as common as those of girls. Boys are a problem in the schools as well as in the streets. A study of 10 cities showed that three out of four students regarded as problem cases by teachers were boys. Because boys are regarded as "problems," teachers are more likely to fail them. More than two out of three students who fail in one or more grades are boys.

Our prisons are overloaded with males. In 1960 only 3 per cent of the felons in state prisons were women. Among males, young boys are most likely to commit crime. Arrests reach a peak at age 16 and tend to decline thereafter.

More troubled by social roles and sex norms, modern men lead rougher lives than women. More is expected of them and their emotional outlets are more limited. They must fight—not cry, tremble, scream or run. They must stay cool, take care of themselves, keep their own counsel. They are under more pressure and have fewer escape valves. Many males are stunted in normal masculine growth and, rebelling against the conspiracy, become outsiders and misfits. For rebel and conformist alike, the stress finally shows in the male's shorter life span—67 years against the female's average of 74.

Baby Fat Floats

Many boys are misfits in schools, as out of place as puppies around the good china. Lately these apathetic and resistant scholars have alarmed schoolmen by organizing protest movements and demanding school reform. We are now forced to ask whether it is the boy or the school that is more maladjusted, and how the dispute between the two can be mediated.

I began this inquiry with the hunch, based on a life spent in classrooms, that boys who rise to the top in school often resemble girls in many important ways. It is the baby fat that usually floats and the muscle that sinks. Scholastic honor and masculinity too often seem incompatible.

We know quite a bit about how boys develop and grow; but at the same time, we have thought very little about masculinity, or about the kind of males we want boys to be. What does it mean to be masculine? It means, obviously, holding male values and following male behavior norms. A boy who follows female norms can confidently be termed less masculine than one who follows male norms. It appears that male norms stress values such as courage, inner direction, certain forms of aggression, autonomy, mastery, technological skill, group solidarity, adventure, and a considerable amount of toughness in mind and body. Of course, a good deal of deviation from these norms is clearly permitted by the male code. (My own father was a professional boxer and athlete, and rather confidently masculine; yet he passed his leisure doing delicate embroidery work and writing poetry.) It is dangerous to attach labels. What is most important is that males be liberated, that they be allowed to be boys and/or to do girlish things, as they choose.

The feminized male is not necessarily a sissy; some are, most are not, though many lean in that direction. Nor is the feminized male a homosexual; some are, most are not. Sex habits may be one thing, and personality quite another. We have simply *not examined* sexual behavior. While we find that many boys and men seem to be acquiring an excess of feminine personality traits, they are not necessarily acquiring a preference for men as sex partners. Many men who have been feminized by the women who rear them remain totally heterosexual in their sex lives.

Schoolmarms

In public elementary schools, 85 per cent of all teachers are women. In all public schools, women are 68 per cent of the total. Men are now a bare majority in secondary schools. Though they are run at the top by men, schools are essentially feminine institutions. Women set the standards for adult behavior, and many favor students who most conform to their own behavior norms—polite, clean, obedient, neat and nice. While there is nothing wrong with this code for those who like it, it does not give boys (or girls either) much room to flex their muscles—physical or intellectual.

The schools mainly teach the words and number symbols of

reading, writing, arithmetic. One hardly ever sees the *things* these symbols stand for. Deeds and actions are rarely the substance of school instruction, activity being viewed as disruptive of academic study.

School words tend to be the words of women. They have their own sound and smell, perfumed or antiseptic. Boys usually prefer tough and colorful short words—while teachers and girls lean toward longer, more floral, opaque synonyms. School words are clean, refined, idealized and as remote from physical things as the typical schoolmarm from the tough realities of ordinary life.

Active word usage, as in *speaking,* is usually discouraged in school; students are expected to speak only when addressed. Even boys who refuse to read or write usually like to talk, but on their own terms. It is the school's most troublesome job to keep boys quiet and in their seats.

Some science is taught in schools, but usually as words detached from things, from doing and discovering. Thus, the magic and adventure of science are missing. Many boys (and girls) with a natural interest in what lies at the heart of physical reality are by-passed.

Feminized Failures

The feminized school simply bores many boys; but it pulls some in one of two opposite directions. If the boy absorbs school values, he may become feminized himself. If he resists, he is pushed toward school failure and rebellion. Increasingly, boys are drawn to female norms. The attraction is the rainbow that lies at the end—graduation with honor, the school diploma, the college degree. As long as employers regard diplomas as *the* badge of merit, boys will be pulled ever deeper into a system that rewards conformity to feminine standards.

Of course, school achievement is not identical with life achievement, though the two are very closely related. Many exceptional boys, of course, can break all school rules and still rise to the top in life. Nor are those who head the most powerful organizations usually the most feminized males. More often they are those who have managed to escape the feminizing influence of school and society.

Urbantown

My initial interest in boys as misfits and feminized males led to a large research effort aimed at finding out what actually happens to boys in school. I wanted to explore three things: how well boys perform in school compared to girls; the relationship between masculinity and school performance; and the characteristics of honor students and of school failures. Urbantown was picked for this study because it contains a typical urban population and because its school system was accessible and of manageable size.

. . .

Comparing masculinity scores with school marks in Urbantown, I found that the more masculine the boy, the lower his report-card average tended to be. Differences among the three groups of boys on this masculinity measure were statistically significant.

The less-masculine boys had better marks in most school subjects. Only in physical education and science did boys with middle-masculinity scores tend to get the best marks. Low-achieving boys got their highest marks in shop and physical education, the two subjects requiring physical rather than verbal skill.

English was the subject in which the greatest disparity was found in the performance of the most masculine boys and the least masculine ones. Relatively speaking, it is the subject in which the most masculine boys have most trouble. In English more than half of the most masculine boys got D's or F's. Half as many of the least masculine boys got such marks.

. . .

Boy Culture

Fish like to swim and boys like to play games. Their craving for games seems insatiable. They exert themselves without fatigue, exhaust themselves without complaint. The boy and young man are so intent on playing games that the school must devote itself to getting them to do what it regards as *work*. So antithetic are work and play, and so separated (one for the class and the other for the playground or gym) that a child who smiles, laughs, talks, or moves about is assumed to be playing and neglecting his work.

A child's natural curiosity is so great that it hardly needs stimulation at school. Rather, it needs acceptance and direction. Instead it usually meets repression and sticky rules that dampen curiosity and take most of the fun out of learning. Boys make astonishing efforts at what interests them. Usually they have trouble sitting still in class —but they sit for hours voluntarily to watch TV, play cards, or work on hobbies. If interested, they *will* learn—eagerly, voluntarily, and without gold stars as incentives.

Clearly we must know more about what interests and motivates boys and about *how* children learn what they want to learn. In particular we need to understand the nature of games and sports so that we may apply their principles (intense group interaction, activity, purpose, clear goals, group competition, problem solving, etc.) to other types of learning. The uses of simulation in learning (enactment of real situations) and games in military and industrial training might give us some useful leads. Women teachers know almost nothing about boy games, and most couldn't care less. For many schoolmarms, sports are the devil that tries to lure the boy away from his work.

"Boy culture" is *not*, we can safely conclude from our findings, identical with school culture. The latter resembles "high culture" and female culture; the former has a distinct identity. Boy culture values machinery and technology. Schools do not.

Boys respond to adults differently from girls. These differences are critical. We found that high achievers in Urbantown try significantly harder to be polite to teachers and to make teachers like them, which may explain why they do so well on teacher evaluations and report-card marks. Thirty-one per cent of the most masculine and 68 per cent of the least masculine try *very* hard to be polite to teachers.

Such response can be interpreted in different ways. Teachers might conclude that low achievers are disrespectful of adults. Some boys might conclude that honor students are apple polishers. Low-achieving boys have an honor code, too—a very strong one. Adults understand very little about this code and certainly do not reward it in the school. An important feature of the code seems to be a group compact that forbids apple polishing or buttering up people you don't really like. It is the small-group equivalent of treason. One does not consort or curry favor with suspected enemies, especially emasculating adult authorities.

Teachers like eager participants, those who speak up in class and give the right answers. Eager students usually are aware that a good way to impress teachers is to enter class discussions. High achievers are much more likely to take part without being called on.

Self-image greatly affects academic performance. Students' views of their own mental capacities can be either crippling or encouraging to them. The major lesson many learn in school is that they are smart or dumb (or gradings in between), depending on marks given them by teachers. Those who are eager come away thinking they must be very smart. After all, they get good marks and are assured that this is a sign of brightness. In fact, good marks seem quite unrelated to real intelligence or ability. Students are convinced that the school *knows* how smart or dumb they are. They are given regular proof in the form of report cards. Such damaging—and fraudulent—"evidence" generates much inarticulate hostility among boys toward school and other authorities.

To Be a Man

Above all else, boys must learn to be strong and independent— to be men. A man must be autonomous, make up his own mind, follow his own direction, without leaning on others too much or asking for too much help. This is a code that is well known to males, but not to females or feminized men.

This drive for independence, perhaps exaggerated in Anglo culture, keeps many men from asking directions when they're lost. It keeps many from going to doctors, especially psychiatrists, when they are sick or unable to cope with trouble. It keeps many males, grown to manhood, from returning to class for literacy training (sitting in a class, they feel, is what children do).

The starkness of the male role is tempered by group camaraderie. Pals and buddies depend on each other and help each other out.

We have seen that relations between many boys and adults in school are not exactly intimate, yet the boys' relations with peers seem strong; these boys spend much of their leisure time with friends, rather than at home with adults. Outside school, they are more likely than others to work and thereby to achieve some financial independence.

Also, they are significantly less likely to turn to parents or others at home for help when they have problems or important decisions to make. In Urbantown, 13 per cent of high, 23 per cent of middle, and 30 per cent of low achievers said they did NOT turn to parents for help. High achievers also spend more time with parents: two out of three high and one out of three low achievers spend more time with parents than with others in their family.

The highest-achieving boys in Urbantown tend to be the babies in the family—either because they are the youngest, only children, or unusually small for their age. Presumably, as a result, they get a good deal of attention from their mothers and are probably favored by them. Many, being youngest siblings, do not acquire the strength and authority of the eldest child. Most come from small families where there are no more than two children, and many have only sisters to play with at home.

Of the 35 boys in Urbantown who are A or A+ students, 19 are the youngest; 11, the eldest; three, in-between; and two are only children.

Cool Fighter

Apparently what boys regard as necessary to masculinity is the willingness to fight on occasion. A boy can be big, strong or athletic, but if he always shrinks from a fight, his reputation as a boy suffers. He apparently doesn't have to be very good at fighting though it helps, but he must have the guts to scrap when he has to. Boys seem to think that the truly masculine boy is quietly strong, cool, not always showing off or testing his masculinity.

If we acknowledge that a certain amount of aggression is desirable and a major resource from which modern society was created, then the problem is not one of suppressing aggression, but of turning it to good uses. Aggression involves a drive to mastery over oneself, others, or the environment. We can use it to fight wars or build cities. We hope to choose the latter.

Aggression can be directed through two major outlets—doing and talking. Girls usually turn to verbal forms, as do many boys. Words are powerful weapons, but they are not substitutes for real tools or for actions. In academic life, words are enshrined to the point that many feel all wars are settled and all deeds accomplished through argument and speech-making.

Verbal aggression is also far from being as safe and civilized as teachers and mothers seem to think. Mean, angry and abrasive words can stir up a lot of trouble. The verbally aggressive can produce their own cultural barbarism—and do. Somehow they assume that, while a physical blow is uncivilized, assaulting people with verbal blows is perfectly fine.

An Unmanly Place

In the organization scheme of things and the system of bosses and underlings, blacks are not the only ones who have been treated as niggers—they are simply the worst victims. Students are also easy targets. Many schools and academies are dehumanizing and unmanly places. Boys who succeed in them often do so by grossly violating many codes of honor and the norms of boy culture.

Mother's Revenge

Having excelled in the schools, girls then confront some of life's realities. In this society and most others, the stark reality is that men hold the best jobs, almost all the power, and most of the privilege and status that really count. It is indeed a man's world.

Many women go at their limited and arduous tasks with a vengeance. Denied the power to give orders on the job, women have developed compensating muscle in the home and school. There a woman has some power over children. A special target has been the males in her family, those who can do what she feels she can't. Sons, easy objects of her creative impulse and desire to shape human destinies and events, are often victims of the female's repressed antagonism and legitimate resentment of male privileges. Her fierce domination of home and school has tended to feminize the men she brings up. Although the exclusion of women from "man's work" has protected certain male privileges, it has also left some unintended marks on men.

The exclusion of women from all the places where important decisions are made has tended to dehumanize and sterilize most of our social institutions and seriously degrade the quality of our lives.

What we must do is masculinize the schools and feminize the power structure of the society—balancing out the sexes so they don't corrode any one spot where they concentrate. A new balance would also familiarize women with the real world. They cannot teach their sons and students much about it when they themselves live in total ignorance of it.

The home is woman's private domain, but it is not always big enough for her. There, in lieu of genuine self-realization she may turn her full effort to the indulgence, domination, and even seduction of her sons. Since few women can sustain such extravagant intimacy, many alternate between love and hostility, giving the anxious impression to their sons that mother may be more antagonist than protector.

While the sons of such mothers may do very well in school, they are often retarded in normal masculine growth and are in conflict with themselves or others. They swell the ranks of the alienated, the withdrawn or rejected, the fearful, the addicted, the feminized.

Many women actively dislike and resent males. They take their revenge where they can, in the home and the school, on the young males they control. They both pamper them and punish them.

Mama is only half the problem. The other half is Papa. Papa's absence from home, his abdication of authority to Mama, his weakness, brutality, or failure to relate to his son can also lead to feminization. Because so many fathers—among the rich, as among the poor —are deficient in one way or another, father substitutes are needed in the schools to give boys a strong taste of what it's like to be an adequate adult male.

The skeptic naturally asks, "If women infect the schools, what happens if they invade other institutions—will they not infect and feminize them too? Wouldn't it be better simply to reduce their influence throughout the society?"

My own answer is unequivocal. Women would not infect these institutions, they would improve them. Women in control posts would increase their responsiveness to human need.

What guarantees have we that women will not feminize the institutions they enter? We have none, no more than we have guarantees for blacks as they come into power. Women will not be sent back to the hearth, nor blacks to the plantation, and a booming economy must consume all available talent.

Bungled Job

What should we teach in the school? All other educational questions hinge on the answer to this one—including how and how long, what kind of buildings, facilities, etc., it should be taught in, and who should do the teaching. I would suggest that people in the schools— the professionals, the administrators, the teachers, and the scholars— are *not* competent to decide what boys should study. They have the job, but they have bungled it.

The first consultant to bring in is the learner himself, since he is the one who must buy the product. The boy can figure in the decisions in several ways. The experts can give him more options about what and how to learn. As it is, the student has little choice. He doesn't even have the options he has on the job—the right to quit, to choose among employers, to work at what pleases him. Given the total compulsion of the schools, it is perhaps remarkable that more boys do not break out.

Who else should decide what is to be taught? As many people as possible, particularly fathers and other males, real men from all walks of life who know the real world.

Manly learning calls for mastery—of self and the environment —and for the expression of outgoing and assertive impulses. It will be active rather than passive, will generate self-control, will demand initiative and much independent work unsupervised by adults and will give students adult responsibilities and rewards whenever possible. It will stop the continuous test-and-evaluation routine that is so humiliating and emasculating. And it will—most importantly— devote itself to stimulating group life and group study to develop a cooperative community and a vehicle for self-help and mutual aid among peers.

Psychologists studying values have found that male values are more theoretical, economic and political—while female values are more esthetic, social and religious. This suggests that boys will be interested in both theoretical and practical things, in making money and achieving power. These interests should be incorporated into the school along with esthetic and social values.

Schools are so thoroughly feminine that even the music suits girls better. Songs, for example, tend to appeal to their tastes and are usually too high-pitched for boy voices. Most forms of self-expression in schools are similarly suited to girls.

It is a grim but common error to assume that boys do not *like* to read. My impression is that most boys, left alone with interesting books and magazines, love to read. But they usually take little pleasure in assigned text reading. Reading books becomes so associated with texts and homework that boys are often ashamed to be seen carrying a book and are even reluctant to admit they like reading.

Expendable Boys

High schools do not want everyone to graduate. Nor do they want everyone to get honors, or even good marks. Teachers understand, because administrators usually tell them, that a certain proportion of students should fail and get poor marks.

In this system, those chosen for failure and the low-mark quotas are often the masculine boys. They are the most expendable, since they are often not "good" boys anyhow.

Nowhere in this system are there many men with whom most boys can identify and say, "I'd like to be like him." Though efforts are made in some places to pick good superintendents and principals, even here alarmingly few are found who can inspire much trust or emulation in male students. Often, like top sergeants, they are least likely to win the loyalties of males who serve under them. They can give orders and, if they use a club, even get them obeyed, but they can rarely reach the will or the spirit of their subordinates.

Another major question that arises is, Should we have more men teachers in the schools? The best answer is probably "yes if"—*if* the men we hire are the kind that boys admire and respect, and if they are intellectual leaders as well as leaders of men. If they are not, they may be worse than women.

Teaching has not been a manly profession, nor school a manly occupation for boys. We have not been able to recruit the best males into teaching. Salaries have been too low, qualifications too arbitrary, and the job too female and lacking in status.

Changes in school jobs and job qualifications would attract more men to teaching. We might want, for example, to set up new school job classifications—such as resource person, or group leader, or technical specialist. Men from the community might perform these jobs. They might be pilots, plumbers, electricians, electronic repairmen, police, politicians, dentists, etc.—anyone with knowledge and skill worth passing on to boys. Group workers, recruited from among even the unskilled males in the community, might spend regular periods with small groups, to counsel with them or assist in recreation.

No Way Out

We cannot flee the schools. Along with their great potential for good, they do too much mischief to children, and we sink too much of our public funds into them to give up. Let us see if we can't reshape them. We have seen that schools *do* influence the behavior of many boys and girls, and that they deepen the hostility of some and docility of others. We have also seen that the schools, and the colleges they feed, are rising swiftly, not declining, in their power over the society they are supposed to serve. They must be watched, vigilantly, not ignored or abandoned.

We need real heroes and we need to think more about what we want our males to be, but mainly we need to step aside and let boys develop like boys. We should encourage their efforts to become strong and autonomous males. Let them run and play like boys, let them learn the things that boys want to learn, let them dress and act like boys. And let's restrain, if we can, the mothers, schools and society that want to dress them up like women or children.

Questions

1. Recall your own school experiences. How did teachers affect male students? Female students? Is college—with a preponderance of male teachers—any different?

2. Beginning with the fourth paragraph, a large number of statistics are quoted. Why? Are you startled by the statistics?

3. Why does Sexton assert that "Murders are usually committed by quiet and gentle men, 'nice guys' "? Are you surprised by this statement?

4. What evidence have you seen to support or refute the idea that "active rebels, as well as the passive hippie protesters," are feminized middle-class boys?

5. How do boys' games differ from girls' games? In what ways do schools encourage and discourage various types of boys' and girls' games?

6. What voice does the author adopt? What thematic structure? How do these affect your willingness to accept what the author says?

7. Do you find it odd that a woman speaks out against "feminizing" boys? Why has the author used the word "feminize" to make her point? Examine the various connotations of the word.

8. Sexton's article is written in serious and almost academic prose. Try to show visually what she says in words by writing a scenario (a shooting script) for a short documentary film on "How the American Boy is Feminized." Indicate what scenes you will film in the school, being very precise about what people will say to each other, what sort of dress those you film will wear, any music you would use, and what the camera will "see" at every point. Make two columns, putting all descriptions of visuals in the left column and all explanations of sounds in the right column beside the corresponding visuals.

The Beige Epoch: Depolarization of Sex Roles in America

CHARLES WINICK

Perhaps the most significant and visible aspect of the contemporary American sexual scene is the tremendous decline, since World War II, in sexual dimorphism. Sex roles have become substantially neutered and environmental differences, increasingly blurred.

Our Age of the Neuter begins to leave its mark on young people in their very tender years. Gender-linked colors like pink and blue for children's clothing are yielding to green, yellow, and other colors which can be used for either Dick or Jane. Such names, however, are less likely nowadays. A study of a large sample of given names reported in birth announcements in the *New York Times* from 1948 to 1963 concluded that almost one-fifth of them were not gender-specific, for example, Leslie, Robin, Tracy, Dana, Lynn, although the 1923–1938 period had few such names.[1] Since the name helps to position a person in his culture, many young people are starting out with an ambisexual given name.

The hair of little girls is shorter and that of little boys is longer, and such blurring is given fashionable designations, that is, the Oliver or Beatle haircut. Other kinds of his-hers appearances are chic for

[1] Charles Winick, *The New People: Desexualization in American Life* (New York: Pegasus, 1968), chap. vi.

young people. Boys and girls may have similar toys, and the last few years have witnessed the popularity of dolls for boys (G.I. Joe and his many imitators).

Reading habits of young people are less related to gender than they were a generation ago. Both sexes are likely to enjoy the same books, for example, *The Moon Spinners* and *Island of the Blue Dolphins*, and there is less interest in books which are clearly sex-linked, like the *Nancy Drew* series for girls or the *Hardy Boys* for boys. School curricula are offering fewer subjects which are unique to each sex, and both sexes learn some subjects; for example, typing.

The Teen-ager

Dating behavior of teen-agers reflects the crossing over of sex roles which pervades so much of the preadolescent years. The teen-age girl increasingly is looking for her own satisfaction and may want to be even more equal than her date. Such tendencies have become more important since the 1950's, which experienced the first movie about a sexually aggressive teen-ager (*Susan Slept Here*, 1954), an extraordinarily successful novel about a sexually sophisticated girl (*Lolita*, 1958), and, perhaps most important, a series of very popular mannequin dolls, beginning with Betsy McCall in 1954 and culminating in Barbie in 1959. Barbie is a sexy teen-ager, and playing with her involves changing costumes and thereby preparing for dates. During the last decade, an average of more than 6,000,000 mannequin dolls was sold each year.

The rehearsal for dating provided by Barbie and her imitators may even further accelerate the social development of their owners. By the time an owner is ready to engage in actual dating, she could be much more forward than her male companion. Studies of teen dating suggest that, not too long ago, the aggressiveness displayed by many contemporary teen-age girls was once found primarily in young men.[2]

So much time separated the nine-year-old with an old-fashioned baby doll from her role as mother that she could enjoy fantasies about motherhood and not be concerned about doing something about them. But the distance in years that separates a Barbie fan from a socially active ten- or eleven-year-old girl is slight, and she

---

[2] Ira L. Reiss, "Sexual Codes in Teen-Age Culture," THE ANNALS, *American Academy of Political and Social Science*, Vol. 338 (November 1961), pp. 53–62.

can easily translate doll-play fantasies into real social life. Barbie owners may be more ready than any previous generation to take the traditional male role in teen-age courtship behavior.

Clothing and Appearance

The most conspicuous example of sexual crisscrossing is provided by clothing and appearance, which are important, because the costume we wear reflects the customs by which we live. When World War II provided an urgent occasion for a re-evaluation of social roles, Rosie the Riveter, in slacks, became a national heroine. At the same time, many of the 14,000,000 men in uniform, who had a limited number of outlets for their money, began to buy fragrance-containing colognes, hair preparations, and after-shave lotion. Wearing the uniform probably helped to allay any fears that the products' users might be unmanly or were indulging themselves.

The most recent postwar impetus for men's fragrance products was the great success of Canoe in 1959. College men traveling abroad began to bring back the sweet and citrus-scented French cologne, used it for themselves—and gave it to their girl friends. The appetite of college students and teen-agers for strongly scented products in turn influenced their fathers, uncles, and older brothers.

Scent is a method of adornment by which a man of any age can unbutton his emotional self and attract attention, in frank recognition of women's growing freedom to pick and choose.[3] Very strong fragrances may have special appeal to men who are suffering from feelings of depersonalization. Just as anointing and incense helped to extend the body's boundaries and reach toward God, a man using a strong fragrance transcends his body's boundaries and creates a unified atmosphere that projects him toward people. Other men who are confused about their body-image may use zesty essences as one way of reassuring themselves, in our deodorized age, that their body is recognizable and has exudations. For these and other reasons, men in the Scented Sixties spend three times as much money on fragrance-containing preparations as women do.

With men smelling so sweet, it is small wonder that the constitutionality of the New York State statute prohibiting a man from wearing a woman's clothes was challenged in 1964 for the first time.

---

[3] Charles Winick, "Dear Sir or Madam, As the Case May Be," *Antioch Review*, Vol. 23 (Spring 1963), pp. 35–49.

Apparel may oft proclaim the man, but many bells are jangling out of tune in the current proclamation. Men are wearing colorful and rakishly epauleted sports jackets, iridescent fabrics, dickies, and bibbed and pleated shirts of fabrics like batiste and voile.

Men's trousers are slimmer and in many instances are worn over girdles of rubber and nylon. Ties are slender and often feminine. The old reliable gray fedora has given way to softer shapes and shades, sometimes topped by gay feathers. Sweaters are less likely to have the traditional V-neck than a boat neck adopted from women's fashions. Padded shoulders on a suit are as out of date as wide lapels and a tucked-in waist. The new look is the soft, slender, straight-line silhouette that also characterizes the shift, which has been the major woman's dress style of the 1960's. Men accessorize their clothes with cuff links, tie bars and tacks, bracelets, rings, and watch bands.

Loss of gender is especially conspicuous in shoes, with women wearing boots or low-heeled, squat, square-toed, and heavy shoes at the same time that men's footwear has become more pointed, slender, colorful, and high-heeled. Men have adopted low-cut and laceless models from women's styles.

A modishly dressed couple might be walking along with the woman in hip-length boots, "basic black" leather coat, a helmet, and a pants suit or straight-line dress of heavy fabric. Her male companion might be wearing a soft pastel sack suit, mauve hat, and a frilled and cuff-linked pink shirt. He could sport a delicate tie and jewelry, exude fragrance, and wear tapered shoes with stacked heels. Both could have shoulder-length hair, and their silhouettes would be quite indistinguishable.

Recreation and Leisure

The couple might be on the way to visit a family billiard center or bowling alley, now that both recreations have become somewhat feminized and have abandoned their connotations of the spittoon. Women are participating in many other previously male recreational activities, especially outdoor sports and competitive athletics. They accounted for 30 per cent of our tennis players in 1946 but today represent 45 per cent. The proportion of women golfers has risen from one-tenth to more than one-third in the same period. The pre-World War II golf club, which did not permit women, has become the family-centered country club. Men's city clubs have also substantially abandoned their formerly exclusionist attitudes toward women.

Social dancing has become almost a misnomer for the self-centered, nonrelational dances which have succeeded the Twist since 1961 and have largely replaced traditional steps like the waltz and fox-trot, in which the man led and the woman followed. In the Frug and Boogaloo and other current favorites, there is no leading or following. The man and woman do not even have to look at each other or start or finish together.

Work and the Home

We are so familiar with decreased resistance to the employment of women and their continually improving preparation for work that we may sometimes forget some implications of the trend. Well over one-third of our workers are women, and, every year, proportionately more married women enter the labor market. Over 2,300,000 women earn more than their husbands. Now that the United States is the first country in which the majority of jobs are in service industries, it has also become the first country where men may soon be competing for what were previously women's jobs.

Men are less and less likely to require physical strength on the job. They are also hardly likely to assume a traditional male role in the home. The husband must often take over household tasks that were once assigned to the wife. Over three-fifths assist in cooking. In many ways, the husband has become a part-time wife. As one result of this trend, initiative and aggressiveness may become less common in boys, who may have less opportunity to see their fathers functioning in either a traditional or masterful manner.

Food and Drink

As Talcott Parsons has so eloquently reminded us, the social structure constitutes a subtly interrelated and almost homeostatic series of interrelationships. At a time when the most basic difference in a society—between men and women—is dwindling, we might expect to find other differences becoming less significant. Extremes of taste sensation in food and drink have diminished as part of our culture's larger homogenization.

Blended whiskey's comparative lack of bouquet and flavor is probably the chief reason for its now accounting for over two-thirds of all domestic whiskey production. The most successful Scotches of the last fifteen years have all been brands which are light amber in color and possess a minimum of maltiness, smokiness, and body.

The dilution of distinguishing characteristics that is represented by "soft" whiskey and Scotch can be seen most dramatically in vodka, which jumped from one per cent of the 1952 domestic liquor market to 10 per cent in 1967. United States government regulations specify that it must be "without distinctive character, aroma or taste," so that its major appeal is a lack of the very qualities that, traditionally, make liquor attractive. Beer is also becoming "lighter" every year.

It would be logical to expect our great technological proficiency to have produced foods with an enormous range of taste, texture, and aroma. Yet our marriage of technology and convenience has led to wide acceptance of many foods with a blander and less explicit taste than in previous generations. Although access to more than 7,000 quick-preparation convenience items has exposed Americans to many new foods, the taste, aroma, and texture of such products tend to be more homogenized and less sharp than the fresh foods of earlier decades, as nonchemically treated fruits, home- or bakery-made bread, ethnic cooking, and many other contributors to strong taste experiences become less common.

Inner and Outer Space

In the Beige Epoch, color extremes are less welcome than they used to be. Even cosmetics stress paleness. The muted appearance of no-color color makes an ideal of "the suddenly, startlingly candid new beauties" whose makeup "turns on the immensely touching *au courant* look of the untouched, nude complexion."[4]

Beige has become the single most popular color for home interiors, carpeting, telephones, draperies. At the same time, interiors are less likely to have the heavy furniture, dark colors, and coarsely grained dark woods generally linked with men or the delicate furniture, light colors, and finely grained light woods that are associated with women.

Rooms with gender may soon be subjects for archaeologists, as a result of the continuing displacement of rooms by areas that merge into one another. And with the near-disappearance of masculine (for example, the leather club model) or feminine (for example, the chaise longue) chairs, foam rubber has become the Space Age's upholstering of choice. It is neutral and has no "give," in contrast to traditional upholstering's indentations after someone has been sitting on it.

---

[4] *Harper's Bazaar,* No. 3041 (April 1965), p. 214.

Our manipulation of outer space, via architecture, reflects the blurring of gender which also characterizes how we use furniture in the organization of inner space. Few clearly feminine (for example, the Taj Mahal) or masculine (for example, the Empire State Building) structures have been built during the last generation. When men and women wear the same straight-line silhouette and are surrounded by furniture which avoids protuberances or padding, it is hardly surprising that their buildings so literally resemble "filing cases for people," although Frank Lloyd Wright intended his famous description to be only a metaphor.

Function is almost as difficult to identify as gender in many new buildings. Hotel, bank, air terminal, lobby, store, office, and restaurant may look alike and play the same monotonous canned music, which provides a seamless wallpaper of sound.

The Performing Arts

Men began to lose their dominant chairs at the head of the formerly rectangular dinner table at just about the time that they were yielding the center spotlight in each of the major performing arts to women. Caruso was the dominant figure of the Golden Age of Opera, but Birgit Nilsson, Joan Sutherland, Renata Tebaldi, Leontyne Price, and Maria Callas are typical of the divas who completely overshadow the male singers opposite whom they appear.

When Actors Equity celebrated its fiftieth birthday in 1963 by enacting some representative episodes from the recent past, not one actor did a major scene.[5] Lillian Gish, Helen Hayes, and Beatrice Lillie were the stars of the evening, performing excerpts from *Our Town, Victoria Regina,* and *Charlot's Review,* respectively. The male matinee idol (E. H. Sothern, John Barrymore, Richard Mansfield, John Drew, Joseph Schildkraut) took his final bow some decades ago. It would be nearly impossible to make up a list of "first men" of the contemporary theatre, but women have dominated our stage for about forty years. Anne Bancroft, Geraldine Page, Kim Stanley, and Julie Harris are only a few younger current Broadway actresses who project characters with valid juices. Aggressive performers like Ethel Merman, Mary Martin, Barbra Streisand, Carol Channing, and Julie Andrews star in musicals which feature male leads who are either

---

[5] Paul Gardner, "3 of Stage's First Ladies Salute Actors Equity on 50th Birthday," *New York Times,* May 6, 1963.

innocuous or nonsingers and are puny successors to the male singers, dancers, and comedians who made the American musical our happiest export.

The interrelationships and mutual reinforcement among the mass media are so pronounced that we might expect women to have assumed much greater importance in movie roles since World War II. Death or retirement claimed Humphrey Bogart, Clark Gable, Spencer Tracy, William Powell, and other actors who shouldered through the "movie movies" of the 1930's. Actresses are now more important than ever before, and Doris Day has played more consecutive starring roles than any performer since talkies began forty years ago. Marilyn Monroe became an unforgettable symbol of the child-woman, and Elizabeth Taylor is not only the highest paid performer in history ($2 million plus for *Cleopatra*) but also the prototype of the devouring Medusa in her private life. As in the earlier case of Ingrid Bergman, Miss Taylor made the key decision to leave one man for another, and both men acquiesced.

One of the most significant changes in the post-World War II performing arts was the emergence in the 1950's of the pianist Liberace as television's first and only superstar who had the qualities of a matinee idol. Liberace was not a particularly distinguished pianist, and much of his appeal seems to lie in his ability to communicate many characteristics of a five- or six-year-old child, of either gender.[6] His extraordinary rise to fame as America's biggest single concert attraction, barely thirty years after the disappearance of the virile stage idol in form-fitting doublet and dashing skin-tight breeches, is a striking commentary on changes in American fantasy needs.

Why Depolarization?

It would be possible to identify many other areas in which our society is manifesting a depolarization and bleaching of differences. Such neutering and role-blurring represent only one dimension in the dynamics of social change. It is possible that these trends necessarily develop in any society which becomes as highly industrialized as ours. There is reason to suspect that our acceptance of androgyny is, to some extent, one outcome of World War II. Studies of children from homes in which the father was absent during the war have suggested

---

[6] Charles Winick, "Fan Mail to Liberace," *Journal of Broadcasting*, Vol. 6 (Spring 1962), pp. 129–142.

that many such children later exhibited considerable sex-role confusion.[7] Large numbers of such children could have been so affected by their fathers' absence and might be significantly represented in the ranks of today's young adults.

A fuller consideration of the conditions and factors producing neutering would include political, economic, technological, cultural, and demographic dimensions as well as rates of invention, acculturation, cultural diffusion, and resistance to change. Our no-war, no-peace situation also contributes to the situation, along with the blurring of categories in other fields.

The unique capacities of each sex are especially significant these days, when at least some quantitative aspects of a Great Society seem within reach. The emancipation of women and their greater equality and participation in the affairs of society were long overdue. But equality does not mean equivalence, and a difference is not a deficiency.

Multivalent, amorphous, and depolarized roles might theoretically lead to increased flexibility and options in behavior, but in actuality may tend to invoke uncertainty. Some tolerance of ambiguity is desirable for a healthy personality, but today's environment and culture are ambiguous enough to tax the adaptability of even the healthiest personalities.[8] The other extreme is represented by the completely polarized sex roles that we associate with the reactionary ideology of totalitarianism.

There is no evidence that any one kind of family structure is inherently healthier than any other, and history seems to suggest that almost any male-female role structure is viable, so long as there is clear division of labor and responsibilities. An equally important lesson of the past is that overly explicit roles can be pathogenic, because they do not permit the expression of individual differences or of a personal style. It is most disquieting to contemplate the possibility that the ambiguity of sex roles in our open society might ultimately prove to be almost as hazardous as the rigidities of authoritarianism.

---

[7] Lois M. Stolz, *Father Relations of War-born Children* (Palo Alto: Stanford University Press, 1951).

[8] T. W. Adorno, E. Frenkel-Brunswik, D. J. Levinson, and R. Nevitt Sanford, *The Authoritarian Personality* (New York: Harper, 1950), pp. 480–481.

Poster Prints

Questions

1. Is it true that a name helps position a person in his culture? How can a name affect your expectations? Does the name Marion Morrison sound more or less masculine than the name John Wayne? (The former is John Wayne's real name.)

2. Do you find it strange that both sexes take some subjects such as typing in school? Or enjoy similar books?

3. Do clothing and appearance define roles, or are they the result of roles?

4. What is Winick's "norm" for masculinity? Is understanding his norm important for coming to grips with his argument? How would the assumptions of someone like Kate Millet differ from those of Winick?

5. Do you agree with Winick's interpretations of his observations? Are his conclusions logically valid? Is he "objective"? Does he respond as a "scientist" analyzing data, or as one using evidence to persuade you of the truth of his point of view?

6. Are styles a good gauge of the trends of masculinity or femininity? What do bland foods and beige rooms have to do with masculinity and femininity?

7. Who are the "heroes" of the modern screen? The "anti-heroes"? How does their sexuality differ? Do you find evidence of "heroines" and "anti-heroines"?

8. In three separate paragraphs, write about a single aspect of the supposed depolarization of sex roles as the matter would be seen from each of the following points of view: traditional masculine, traditional feminine, and one which rejects distinctions by sex. Be careful to alter your writing voice to fit the views and attitudes of a person holding each point of view.

The Brief Rebellion
of the American Male

ARNOLD M. AUERBACH

The American Male awoke feeling troubled. Another bright, brisk young magazine writer was to interview him this morning. "The American Male in Close-up," the piece was to be called, inevitably. Subtitle: "A Long Hard Look at All Previous Long Hard Looks."

He got out of bed slowly. Already he could see the article in print and feel the old familiar brickbats bouncing off his head.

He shuffled into the bathroom and looked at his aging English-French-Scandinavian-Irish features in the mirror. Hair a bit thinner; neck muscles seemed somewhat saggier, too. He brushed his teeth with his electric toothbrush, cheered by the reflection that he had 45 per cent fewer cavities and 8 per cent more teeth than last century.

He shaved, showered, wrapped a towel around his middle, and went back to the bedroom. He looked down at his sleeping wife, the American Female. She was frowning a bit—not, he had to admit, her most becoming expression. He wondered uneasily if she *did* dominate him. He'd seen enough TV situation comedies to know his image: a bumbling oaf, ruled by a Wise Better Half and their Adorable Nippers.

Still, if the Female *did* dominate him, he hadn't noticed. After all, when he sounded off, she still listened, or *seemed* to. But that might be one of her Female tricks. And now that she owned more common stock than he did, she might have moved in on him, hardheaded-wise.

He sat on the edge of the bed, pondering. Seemed as if someone was *always* dominating him. Not long ago it had been his American Mom. But he'd snipped the silver cord, by God, and put Mom in her place. Nobody even wrote songs about her anymore. Mom was a Senior Citizen now, with bright-gold hair and a low cholesterol count. He sighed. Not much point escaping from one tyrant merely to fall into the clutches of another, was there? He put on his underwear and stared in frustration at the Female. She opened her eyes.

"Something's bothering you," she said.

"Nothing's bothering me at all," he said crossly.

The Female sat up and smiled. "It's that interview, isn't it? Stop feeling sorry for yourself. They pick on me, too," she said, and went downstairs to make breakfast.

He felt a twinge of guilt. She was right. Critics had given *her* the treatment, too. Predatory, they'd called her, and Frigid and even, of late (he hitched up his shorts defensively), a Castrator. It was a wonder she had any Feminine Mystique left. He looked at his watch. Time for the morning news. He turned on the little bedside radio. As usual, the bulletins spoke of tension in far-off lands with unfamiliar names, and he wondered what had happened to the places he'd known so well during those world wars. Seemed as if the minute you learned one set of trouble spots, another sprang up. One consolation, though: he'd outgrown that isolationist stuff. This was One World now—and he owned a Volkswagen and a Japanese camera to prove it.

But he knew he was still politically naïve. He remained Uncle Sugar and Uncle Shylock; he was Yankee (and Yanqui) Go Home; he was a Saber Rattler and a Rocket Rattler, with a Gangster Mentality; he was a Dollar Diplomat and a Well-meaning Blunderer; he was the Ugly American, the Loud-mouthed American, and the Offensive Tourist. The American Male shook his head glumly. He was 38 per cent better educated this century, and getting more schooling every year; time to profit by his added knowledge. Guiltily he recalled that a Frenchman had recently estimated his mental age as thirteen. Well, at that, thirteen was an improvement; it used to be twelve.

He snapped off the radio and put on his other-directed, conformist suit. Then, about to tie his tie, he eyed his wallet—symbol of loathsome affluence. In it were the things he was always chasing —Fast Bucks! And Fast Bucks (as distinguished from quaint, old-fashioned Slow Bucks) were his sordid reward for hooking his knee into the groin of other American Males. To do otherwise made you an *Un*-American Male.

But the wallet contained further proof of his shifty, expense-account morality—a Diners' Club card. Lurking in it were yet other mortifying data: Social Security and Blue Cross cards, driver's license, office pass. Were some cards counter-punched? Did they bear complex serial numbers and code letters? Crushing evidence of his lack of identity in an Orwellian, automated society.

The American Male cringed. He was a Man in a Gray Flannel Suit in a Split-level Trap; he was a Fat Cat and a Dog-eating Dog; he was faceless, graceless, and Big Brother-watched; he was a rat-racing, buck-chasing Babbitt. He was a Lousy Lover. (Nope; that was the Latins, thank God.) He picked up his car keys and dropped them in disgust. They bespoke his vulgar relaxations—Sundays when he and his family, scorning the Volkswagen, climbed into their chrome-laden Detroit status symbol, to clog the highways and spread fumes, smog, and litter.

He sank despondently into an Eames chair, seeking a return to the womb. He sat a moment in numb silence. Then as he heard loud voices down the hall, he groaned. His children, the American Teen-ager and the American Pre-adolescent, were quarreling again. Here was final proof of his inadequacy. He pondered the American Teen-ager—delinquent, neurotic, rebellious without a cause, increasingly prone to get pregnant (or to impregnate), more and more susceptible to the hasty marriage and the ghastly divorce. And the American Pre-adolescent—insecure, coddled, compulsively competing in Little Leagues and ballet classes, hopelessly vacillating between schools overstructured and overprogressive. His mind reeled.

Perhaps, as psychologists charged, he and the Female had wor-shiped the children too much, using them as mere ego-gratification symbols. But in ancient Rome, some Mom (Cordelia? Cornelia, that was it) had been immortalized for saying of her offspring, "These are my jewels." In olden times, apparently, showing off the brats was heroic. Today it gave them traumas.

Down the hall, the voices rose jarringly. The topic seemed to be possession of the bathroom. "I got here *first*," shrieked the American Pre-adolescent (Female). "But I have to shave!" whined her brother, the American Teen-ager. He shuddered. With two such

monsters around the house, he was lucky that the oldest, the American College Student, was away at college. Lucky? No, negligent! For the College Student, as everyone knew, was the most rudderless ship of all: pot-smoking, drop-outing, simultaneously a wastrel and a crass materialist, with morals so loose that they'd soon slip to the floor entirely.

The American Male writhed in his chair. He saw that he and the Female, zeros as mates, had been minuses as parents. They weren't even up on the latest theories; they hadn't read that new best-seller, *Sex and the Unmarried Infant*. And if they had? He recalled that in covered wagons, hammocks, rumble seats, or jets, his children had never stopped spooning, necking, petting, or making out. No matter how parents played it. Youth was eternally Lost, Disillusioned, Beat, Angry, Flaming, or Cool. Had he and the Female been to permissive? But only yesterday they'd been Repressed Victorians.

Down the hall, the quarrel grew more heated. "Beat it, slob!"

"Quit pushing, stupid!" The American Male rose and poked his head out. "Keep those voices down," he called irritably. No letup. As usual, the generations had failed to communicate. He slammed the bedroom door. Abruptly, awareness of his many past misdeeds overwhelmed him. He sank back into his chair.

He'd been no good from the beginning. He'd grabbed his land from the Indians, giving them whiskey and venereal disease in return; he'd drained its resources and despoiled its beauty; he'd fought foolish, bloody wars and botched the peace settlements. Lately, inept as ever, he'd flubbed slum clearance, old-age care, civil rights. Yes, through the years, he'd drifted from one excess to another. He'd been slave trader, fratricide, robber baron, imperialist, speculator, and swiller of bathtub gin. And today, instead of maturing after nearly two centuries, he'd become a foolish, softheaded stereotype. Come to think of it, aside from inventing apple pie and air conditioning, what had he ever done *right?*

And all at once his course was plain. Why go to the office and face another pummeling from the bright, brisk young man? He'd knock off—lie around, putter in the garage, maybe do-it-himself a bit, and let the Female dominate him. Hell, he might even absorb a little packaged culture—a Luce publication or a Book of the Month.

He got up slowly and made his way downstairs. And there, in the kitchen doorway, he paused. The scene before him was bright. The American Female, in her immemorial fashion, was at the stove, frying bacon; coffee was perking; his children, in *their* immemorial fashion, had made peace and beaten him downstairs. Indeed the American Teen-ager had already kidnaped the morning paper and was spreading jam over the sports page; the American Pre-adolescent was hacking with a fork at the dotted lines of a breakfast-food cartoon. In a corner, their American Dog dozed smugly.

The American Male stood in the doorway. Perhaps he'd taken too grim a view of things. True, he'd goofed and would goof again. But the kitchen was sunny, the children had combed their hair, and the bacon looked crisp. Maybe he could get through the interview after all. He entered the kitchen. The American Teen-ager looked up casually from the newspaper. "How you doing, Dad?" he asked.

"I'll live," said the American Male.

Questions

1. Why does the writer call the main character "the American Male" throughout?

2. Is the author correct in saying that the TV image of "the American Male" is that of "a bumbling oaf, ruled by a Wise Better Half and their Adorable Nippers"? What is the TV image of the American female? How do you suppose these images came about?

3. Does this essay define "the American Male"? Is that the purpose of the article? Why are all the "facts" and "statistics" about "the American Male" included?

4. Do your father and the men you know fit this description?

5. What effect does the ending have on what has been said earlier?

6. How does your point of view toward your parents and their actions differ from their point of view toward themselves and what they do? Their point of view and yours to what you are and do? Is the difference simply one of age? From the point of view of one of your parents, write a letter to your "daughter" or "son" dealing with a subject you have talked about frequently together. Take your parent's point of view seriously and try to present it convincingly.

7. Compose a humorous essay about the American male or female teenager in which you either show how he or she is unfairly treated at home or in which you demonstrate how his or her condition does not deserve complaint.

The Male Revolt Against Polygyny

(FROM THE PREFACE TO *Getting Married*)

GEORGE BERNARD SHAW

Experience shows that women do not object to polygyny when it is customary: on the contrary, they are its most ardent supporters. The reason is obvious. The question, as it presents itself in practice to a woman, is whether it is better to have, say, a whole share in a tenth-rate man or a tenth share in a first-rate man. Substitute the word Income for the word Man, and you will have the question as it presents itself economically to the dependent woman. The woman whose instincts are maternal, who desires superior children more than anything else, never hesitates. She would take a thousandth share, if necessary, in a husband who was a man in a thousand, rather than have some comparatively weedy weakling all to herself. It is the comparatively weedy weakling, left mateless by polygyny, who objects. Thus, it was not the women of Salt Lake City nor even of America who attacked Mormon polygyny. It was the men. And very naturally. On the other hand, women object to polyandry, because polyandry enables the best women to monopolize all the men, just as polygyny enables the best men to monopolize all the women. That is why all our ordinary men and women are unanimous in defence of the monogamy, the men because it excludes polygyny, and the women because it excludes polyandry. The women, left to themselves, would tolerate polygyny. The men, left

Reprinted by permission of the Society of Authors, on behalf of the Bernard Shaw Estate.

to themselves, would tolerate polyandry. But polygyny would condemn a great many men, and polyandry a great many women, to the celibacy of neglect. Hence the resistance any attempt to establish unlimited polygyny always provokes, not from the best people, but from the mediocrities and the inferiors. If we could get rid of our inferiors and screw up our average quality until mediocrity ceased to be a reproach, thus making every man reasonably eligible as a father and every woman reasonably desirable as a mother, polygyny and polyandry would immediately fall into sincere disrepute, because monogamy is so much more convenient and economical that nobody would want to share a husband or a wife if he (or she) could have a sufficiently good one all to himself (or herself). Thus it appears that it is the scarcity of husbands or wives of high quality that leads woman to polygyny and men to polyandry, and that if this scarcity were cured, monogamy, in the sense of having only one husband or wife at a time (facilities for changing are another matter), would be found satisfactory.

Questions

1. Is Shaw serious? Is he trying to be outrageous? To make the reader see an old problem in a new light?

2. Do communes create the state of polygamy Shaw describes?

3. What assumptions does Shaw make about pair-bonding? Do you think his assumptions are valid?

4. Is polygamy worthwhile to consider in light of the apparent deterioration of marriage in America? How would polygamy alter the way people perceive their masculine and feminine identities?

Slam the Door Softly

CLARE BOOTHE LUCE

The scene is the Thaw Wald's cheerfully furnished middle-class living room in New York's suburbia. There are a front door and hall, a door to the kitchen area, and a staircase to the bedroom floor. Two easy chairs and two low hassocks with toys on them, grouped around a television, indicate a family of four. Drinks are on a bar cart at one end of a comfortable sofa, and an end table at the other. There are slightly more than the average number of bookshelves. The lamps are on, but as we don't hear the children, we know it is the Parents' Hour.

As the curtain rises, Thaw Wald, a good-looking fellow, about 35, is sitting in one of the easy chairs, smoking and watching TV. His back is to the sofa and staircase, so he does not see his wife coming down the stairs. Nora Wald is a rather pretty woman of about 32. She is carrying a suitcase, handbag and an armful of books.

Thaw switches channels, and lands in the middle of a panel show, During the TV dialogue that follows Nora somewhat furtively deposits her suitcase in the hall, takes her coat out of the hall closet, and comes back to the sofa carrying coat, purse and books. She lays her coat on the sofa, and the books on the end table. The books are full of little paper slips—bookmarkers. All of the above actions are unobserved by Thaw. We cannot see the TV screen, but we hear the voices of four women, all talking excitedly at once.

THAW. (*To the screen and the world in general.*) God, these Liberation gals! Still at it.

MALE MODERATOR'S VOICE. (*Full of paternal patience wearing a bit thin.*) Ladies! Lay-deez! Can't we switch now from the question of the sex-typing of jobs to what the Women's Liberation Movement thinks about—

OLDER WOMAN'S VOICE. May I finish! In the Soviet Union 83% of the dentists, 75% of the doctors and 37% of the lawyers are women. In Poland and Denmark—

MODERATOR. I think you have already amply made your point, Mrs. Epstein—anything men can do, women can do better!

YOUNG WOMAN'S VOICE. (*Angrily.*) That was *not* her point—and you know it! What she said was, there are very few professional jobs men are doing that women couldn't do, if only—

THAW. Well, for God's sake then, shuddup, and go do 'em—

BLACK WOMAN'S VOICE. What she's been saying, what we've all been saying, and you men just don't want to hear us, is—things are the same for women as they are for us black people. We try to get up, you just sit down on us, like a big elephant sits down on a bunch of poor little mice.

MODERATOR. Well, sometimes moderators have to play the elephant, and sit down on one subject in order to develop another. As I was about to say, ladies, there *is one thing* a woman can do, no man can do—(*In his best holy-night-all-is-bright voice.*) give birth to a *child.*

YOUNG WOMAN'S VOICE. So what else is new?

THAW. One gets you ten, she's a Lesbo—

MODERATOR. (*Forcefully.*) And *that* brings us to marriage! Now, if *I* may be permitted to get in just *one* statistic, edgewise: two thirds of all adult American females are married women. And now! (*At last he's got them where he wants them.*) What *is* the

Women's Lib view of Woman's No. 1 job—Occupation House-wife?

THAW.   Ha! That's the one none of 'em can handle—

YOUNG WOMAN'S VOICE.   (*Loud and clear.*) Marriage, as an institution, is as thoroughly corrupt as prostitution. It is, in fact, legalized and romanticized prostitution. A woman who marries is selling her sexual services and domestic services for permanent bed and board—

BLACK WOMAN'S VOICE.   There's no human being a man can buy anymore—except a woman—

THAW.   (*Snapping off the TV.*) Crrr-ap! Boy, what a bunch of battle-axes! (*He goes back to studying his TV listings.*)

NORA.   (*Raising her voice.*) Thaw! I'd like to say something about what they just said about marriage—

THAW.   (*In a warning voice.*) Uh-uh, Nora! We both agreed months ago, you'd lay off the feminist bit, if I'd lay off watching Saturday football—

NORA.   And do something with the children . . . But Thaw, there's something maybe, I ought to try to tell you myself—(*Thaw is not listening. Nora makes a "what's the use" gesture, then opens her purse, takes out three envelopes, carefully inserts two of them under the covers of the top two books.*)

THAW.   Like to hear Senators Smithers, Smethers and Smothers on "How Fast Can We Get Out of Vietnam?"

NORA.   (*Cool mockery.*) That bunch of pot-bellied, bald-headed old goats! Not one of them could get a woman—well, yes, maybe for two dollars.

THAW.   You don't look at Senators, Nora. You listen to them.

NORA.   (*Nodding.*) Women are only to look at. Men are to listen to. Got it. (*Thaw snaps off the TV. He is now neither looking at her nor listening to her, as he methodically turns pages of the magazine he has picked up.*)

THAW.   Finished reading to the kids?

NORA.   I haven't been reading to the children. I've been reading to myself—and talking to myself—for a long time now.

THAW.   That's good. (*She passes him, carrying the third envelope, and goes into kitchen. Then, unenthusiastically.*) Want some help with the dishes?

NORA'S VOICE.   I'm not doing the dishes.

THAW.   (*Enthusiastically.*) Say, Nora, this is quite an ad we've got in LIFE for Stone Mountain Life Insurance.

NORA'S VOICE. Yes, I saw it. Great. (*She comes back and goes to sofa.*)

THAW. It's the kind of ad that grabs you. This sad-faced, nice-looking woman of 50, sitting on a bench with a lot of discouraged old biddies, in an employment agency. Great captions—(*Reading.*)

NORA AND THAW. (*Together.*) "Could this happen to *your* wife?"

NORA. I'll let you know the answer very shortly. (*A pause.*) You really don't hear me anymore, do you? (*He really doesn't. She buttons herself into her coat, pulls on her gloves.*) Well, there are enough groceries for a week. All the telephone numbers you'll need and menus for the children are in the envelope on the spindle. A girl will come in to take care of them after school—until your mother gets here.

THAW. Uh-huh. . . .

NORA. (*Looks around sadly.*) Well, goodby dear little doll house. Goodby dear husband. You've had the best ten years of my life. (*She goes to the staircase, blows two deep kisses upstairs, just as Thaw glances up briefly at her, but returns automatically to his magazine. Nora picks up suitcase, opens the door, goes out, closing it quietly.*)

THAW. (*Like a man suddenly snapping out of a hypnotic trance.*) Nora? Nora? NOR-RA! (*He is out of the door in two seconds.*)

THAW'S AND NORA'S VOICES. Nora, where're you going?—I'll miss my train—I don't understand—it's all in my letter—let me go!—You come back—(*They return. He is pulling her by the arm. He yanks the suitcase away from her, drops it in the hall.*)

NORA. Ouch! You're hurting me!

THAW. Now what is this all about? (*He shoves her into the room, then stands between her and door.*) Why the hell . . . What're you sneaking out of the house . . . What's that suitcase for?

NORA. I wasn't sneaking. I told you. But you weren't listening.

THAW. I was listening . . . it just didn't register. You said you were reading to yourself. Then you started yakking about the kids and the groceries and the doll house mother sent . . . (*Flabbergasted.*) Goodby?! What do you mean, *goodby?!*

NORA. Just that. I'm leaving you. (*Pointing to books.*) My letter will explain everything—

THAW. Have you blown your mind?

NORA. Thaw, I've got to scoot, or I'll miss the eight-o-nine.

THAW. You'll miss it. (*He backs her to the sofa, pushes her onto it, goes and slams the door and strides back.*) Now, my girl, explain this—

NORA. You mean what's just happened now?

THAW. Yes. What's happened now.

NORA. Oh, that's easy. Muscle. You're made with the muscle—like a typical male. The heavier musculature of the male is a secondary sexual characteristic. Although that's not certain. It could be just the result of selective breeding. In primitive times, of course, the heavier musculature of the male was necessary to protect the pregnant female and the immobile young—

THAW. (*His anger evaporates.*) Nora, are you sick?

NORA. But what's just happened now shows that nothing has changed—I mean, fundamentally changed—in centuries, in the relations between the sexes. *You* still Tarzan, *me* still Jane.

THAW. (*Sits on sofa beside her, feels her head.*) I've noticed you've been . . . well . . . acting funny lately. . . .

NORA. Funny?

THAW. Like there was something on your mind. . . . Tell me, what's wrong, sweetheart? Where does it hurt?

NORA. It hurts (*Taps head.*) here. Isn't that where thinking hurts *you?* No. You're used to it. I was, too, when I was at Wellesley. But I sort of stopped when I left. It's really hard to think of anything else when you're having babies.

THAW. Nora, isn't it about time for your period?

NORA. But if God had wanted us to think just with our wombs, why did He give us a brain? No matter what men say, Thaw, the female brain is not a vestigial organ, like a vermiform appendix.

THAW. Nora . . .

NORA. Thaw, I can just about make my train. I'll leave the car and keys in the usual place at the station. Now, I have a very important appointment in the morning. (*She starts to rise.*)

THAW. Appointment? (*Grabs her shoulders.*) Nora, look at me! You weren't sneaking out of the house to . . . get an abortion?

NORA. When a man can't explain a woman's actions, the first thing he thinks about is the condition of her uterus. Thaw, if you were leaving me and I didn't know why, would I ask, first thing, if you were having prostate trouble?

THAW. Don't try to throw me off the track, sweetie! Now, if you want another baby . . .

NORA. Thaw, don't you remember, we both agreed about the overpopulation problem—

THAW.   To hell with the overpopulation problem. Let Nixon solve that. Nora, I can swing another baby—

NORA.   Maybe you can. I can't. For me there are no more splendid, new truths to be learned from scanning the contents of babies' diapers. Thaw, I *am* pregnant. But not in a feminine way. In the way only men are supposed to get pregnant.

THAW.   Men, pregnant?

NORA.   (*Nodding.*) With ideas. Pregnancies there (*Taps his head.*) are masculine. And a very superior form of labor. Pregnancies here (*Taps her tummy.*) are feminine—a very inferior form of labor. That's an example of male linguistic chauvinism. Mary Ellmann is *great* on that. You'll enjoy her *Thinking about Women.* . . .

THAW.   (*Going to telephone near bookshelf.*) I'm getting the doctor. (*Nora makes a dash for the door, he drops the phone.*) Oh, no, you don't! (*He reaches for her as she passes, misses. Grabs her ponytail and hauls her back by it, and shoves her into the easy chair.*)

NORA.   Brother, Millett sure had you taped.

THAW.   Milly *who?* (*A new thought comes to him.*) Has one of your goddamgossipyfemale friends been trying to break up our marriage? (*He suddenly checks his conscience. It is* not *altogether pure.*) What did she tell you? That she saw me having lunch, uh, dinner, with some girl?

NORA.   (*Nodding to herself.*) Right on the button!

THAW.   Now, Nora, I can explain about that girl—

NORA.   You don't have to. Let's face it. Monogamy is not natural to the male—

THAW.   You know I'm not in love with anybody but you—

NORA.   Monogamy is not natural to the female, either. Making women think it is, is the man's most successful form of brainwashing the female—

THAW.   Nora I swear, that girl means nothing to me—

NORA.   And you probably mean nothing to her. So whose skin is off whose nose?

THAW.   (*Relieved, but puzzled.*) Well, uh, I'm glad you feel that way about—uh—things.

NORA.   Oh, it's not the way I *feel.* It's the way things really are. What with the general collapse of the mores, and now the Pill, women are becoming as promiscuous as men. It figures. We're educated from birth to think of ourselves just as man-traps. Of course, in my mother's day, good women thought of themselves as private man-traps. Only bad women were public man-traps. Now we've all gone public. (*Looks at watch.*) I'll have to take the eight-forty. (*She gets out of her coat, lays it, ready to slip into, on back of sofa.*)

THAW. (*A gathering suspicion.*) Nora, are you trying to tell me . . . that *you*—

NORA. Of course, a lot of it, today, is the fault of the advertising industry. Making women think they're failures in life if they don't make like sex-pots around the clock. We're even supposed to wear false eyelashes when we're vacuuming. Betty Friedan's great on that. She says many lonely suburban housewives, unable to identify their real problem, think more sex is the answer. So they sleep with the milkman, or the delivery boy. If I felt like sleeping with anybody like that, I'd pick the plumber. When you need *him,* boy you *need* him!

THAW. (*The unpleasant thought he has been wrestling with has now jelled.*) Nora . . . are you . . . trying to tell me you are leaving me—for someone else?

NORA. Why, Thaw Wald! How could you even *think* such a thing? (*To herself.*) Now, how naïve can I be? What else do men think about, in connection with women, *but* sex? He is saying to himself, she's not having her period, she's not pregnant, she's not jealous: it's *got* to be another man.

THAW. Stop muttering to yourself, and answer my question.

NORA. I forgot what it was. Oh, yes. *No.*

THAW. No what?

NORA. No, I'm not in love with anybody else. I was a virgin when I married you. And intacta. And that wasn't par for the course—even at Wellesley. And I've never slept with anybody else, partly because I never wanted to. And partly because, I suppose, of our family's Presbyterian hangup. So, now that all the vital statistics are out of the way, I'll just drive around until—(*Begins to slip her arms into coat. He grabs coat, throws it on easy chair.*)

THAW. You're not leaving until you tell me *why.*

NORA. But it's all in my letter. (*Points.*) The fat one sticking out of Simone de Beauvoir's *Second Sex*—

THAW. If you have a bill of particulars against me, I want it—straight. From you.

NORA. Oh, darling, I have no bill of particulars. By all the standards of our present-day society, you are a very good husband.

And, mark me, you'll be president of Stone Mountain Life Insurance Company before you're 50. The point is, what will I be when I'm 50—

THAW. You'll be my wife, if I have anything to say. Okay. So you're not leaving me because I'm a bad husband, or because my financial future is dim.

NORA. No. Oh, Thaw, you just wouldn't understand.

THAW. (*Patiently.*) I might, if you would try, for just one minute, to talk logically—

NORA. Thaw, women aren't trained to talk logically. Men don't like women who talk logically. They find them unfeminine—aggressive—

THAW. Dammit, Nora, will you talk sense . . .

NORA. But boy! does a man get sore when a woman won't talk logically when *he* wants her to, and (*Snaps fingers.*) like that! And *that* isn't illogical? What women men are! Now, if you will step aside—

THAW. (*Grabbing her and shaking her.*) You're going to tell me why you're walking out on me, if I have to *sock* you!

NORA. Thaw, eyeball to eyeball, *I am leaving you*—and not for a man. For reasons of my own I just don't think you *can* understand. And if you mean to stop me, you'll have to beat me to a pulp. But I'm black and blue already.

THAW. (*Seizes her tenderly in his arms, kisses her.*) Nora, sweetheart! You know I couldn't really hurt you. (*Kisses, Kisses.*) Ba-aaby, what do you say we call it a night? (*Scoops her up in his arms.*) You can tell me *all* about it in bed . . .

NORA. The classical male one-two. Sock 'em and screw 'em.

THAW. (*Dumping her on sofa.*) Well, it's been known to work on a lot of occasions. Something tells me this isn't one of them. (*Pours a drink.*)

NORA. I guess I need one, too. (*He mixes them.*) Thaw?

THAW. Yes.

NORA. I couldn't help being a *little* pleased when you made like a caveman. It shows you really do value my sexual services.

THAW. Geez!

NORA. Well, it can't be my domestic services—you don't realize, yet, what they're worth. (*Drinks.*) Thaw, you do have a problem with me. But you can't solve it with force. And *I* do have a problem. But I can't solve it with sex.

THAW. Could you, would you, *try* to tell me what my-you-our problem is?

NORA. Friedan's *Feminine Mystique* is very good on The Problem. I've marked all the relevant passages. And I've personalized them in my letter—(*He goes to book. Yanks out letter, starts to tear it up. Nora groans. He changes his mind, and stuffs it in his pocket.*)

THAW. Look, Nora, there's one thing I've always said about you. For a woman, you're pretty damn honest. Don't you think you owe it to me to level and give me a chance to defend myself?

NORA. The trouble is, *you* would have to listen to *me*. And that's hard for you. I *understand why*. Not listening to women is a habit that's been passed on from father to son for generations. You could almost say, tuning out on women is another secondary sexual male characteristic.

THAW. So our problem is that *I* don't listen?

NORA. Thaw, you always go on talking, no matter how hard I'm interrupting.

THAW. Okay. You have the floor.

NORA. Well, let's begin where this started tonight. When you oppressed me, and treated me as an inferior—

THAW. I oppressed . . . (*Hesitates.*) Lay on, MacDuff.

NORA. You honestly don't think that yanking me around by my hair and threatening to sock me are not the oppressive gestures of a superior male toward an inferior female?

THAW. For Chrissake, Nora, a man isn't going to let the woman he loves leave him, if he can stop her!

NORA. Exactly. Domination of the insubordinate female is an almost instinctive male reflex. *In extremis,* Thaw, it is *rape.* Now, would I like it if you should say you were going to leave me? No. But could I drag you back—

THAW. You'd just have to crook your little finger.

NORA. Flattery will get you nowhere this evening. So, where was I?

THAW. I am a born rapist.

NORA. Wasn't that what you had in mind when you tried to adjourn this to our bedroom? But that's just your primitive side. There's your civilized side too. You are a patriarchal *paterfamilias.*

THAW. What am I now?

NORA. Thaw, you do realize we all live in a patriarchy, where men govern women by playing sexual politics?

THAW. Look, you're not still sore because I talked you into voting for Nixon? (*She gives him a withering look.*) Okay. So we all live in a patriarchy . . .

NORA. Our little family, the Walds, are just one nuclear patriarchal unit among the millions in our patriarchal male-dominated civilization, which is worldwide. It's all in that book—

THAW. Look Nora, I promise I'll read the damn book—but . . .

NORA. So who's interrupting? Well, Thaw, all history shows that the hand that cradles the *rock* has ruled the world, *not* the hand that rocks the cradle! Do you know what brutal things men have done to women? Bought and sold them like cattle. Bound their feet at birth to deform them—so they couldn't run away—like in China. Made widows throw themselves on the funeral pyres of their husbands, like in India. And men who committed adultery were almost never punished. But women were always brutally punished. Why, in many countries unfaithful wives were *stoned* to death—

THAW. This is America, 1970, Nora. And here, when wives are unfaithful, *husbands* get stoned. (*Drinks.*) Mind if I do?

NORA. Be your guest. Oh, there's no doubt that relations between the sexes have been greatly ameliorated . . .

THAW. Now, about *our* relations, Nora. You're not holding it against *me* that men, the dirty bastards, have done a lot of foul things to women in the past?

NORA. (*Indignant.*) What do you mean, in the *past?*

THAW. (*Determined to be patient.*) Past, present, future—what has what other men have done to other women got to do with us?

NORA. Quite a lot. We *are* a male and a female—

THAW. That's the supposition I've always gone on. But Nora, we are a *particular* male and a *particular* female: Thaw Wald and his wife, Nora—

NORA. Yes. That's why it's so shattering when you find out you are such a typical husband and—

THAW. (*A new effort to take command.*) Nora, how many men do you know who are still in love with their wives after ten years?

NORA. Not many. And, Thaw, listen, maybe the reason is—

THAW. So you agree that's not typical? Okay. Now, do I ever grumble about paying the bills? So that's not typical. I liked my mother-in-law, even when she was alive. And God knows that's not typical. And don't I do every damn thing I can to keep *my* mother off your back? And that's not typical. I'm even thought-ful about the little things. You said so yourself, remember, when I bought you that black see-through nightgown for Mother's Day. That I went out and chose myself. And which *you* never wear.

NORA.   I had to return it. It was too small. And do you know what the saleswoman said? She said, "Men who buy their wives things in this department are in love with them. But why do they all seem to think they are married to midgets?" That's it, Thaw, that's *it!* Men "think little"—like "thinking thin"—even about women they love. They don't think at all about women they don't love or want to sleep with. Now, I can't help it if you think of me as a midget. But don't you see, I've got to stop thinking of myself as one. Thaw, *listen* . . .

THAW.   Why the devil should *you* think of yourself as a midget? *I* think you're a great woman. A *real* woman! Why, you're the dearest, sweetest, most understanding little wife—most of the time—a man ever had. And the most intelligent and wonderful little mother! Dammit, those kids are the smartest, best-behaved, most self-reliant little kids . . .

NORA.   Oh, I've been pretty good at Occupation Housewife, if I do say so myself. But, Thaw, *listen.* Can't you even imagine that there might be something *more* a woman needs and wants—

THAW.   My God, Nora, what more can a woman want than a nice home, fine children and a husband who adores her?

NORA.   (*Discouraged.*) You sound like old Dr. Freud, in person.

THAW.   I sound like Freud? I wish I were. Then I'd know why you're so uptight.

NORA.   Oh, no you wouldn't. Know what Freud wrote in his diary, when he was 77? "What do women want? My God, what do they want?" Fifty years this giant brain spends analyzing wom-en. And he still can't find out what they want. So this makes him the world's greatest expert on feminine psychology? (*She starts to look at her watch.*) To think I bought him, in college.

THAW.   You've got plenty of time. You were saying about Freud— (*He lights a cigarette, hands it to her, determined to stick with it to the end.*)

NORA.   History is full of ironies! Freud was the foremost exponent of the theory of the natural inferiority of women. You know, "Anatomy is destiny"?

THAW.   I was in the School of Business, remember?

NORA. Well, old Freud died in 1939. He didn't live to see what happened when Hitler adopted his theory that "anatomy is destiny." Six million of his own people went to the gas chambers. One reason, Hitler said, that the Jews were *naturally* inferior was because they were effeminate people, with a slave mentality. He said they were full of those vices which men always identify with women—when they're feeling hostile: You know, sneakiness and deception, scheming and wheedling, whining and pushiness, oh, and materialism, sensuousness and sexuality. Thaw, what's *your* favorite feminine vice?

THAW. At this moment, feminine monologues.

NORA. I didn't think you'd have the nerve to say sneakiness. I saw you sneak a look at your watch, and egg me on to talk about Freud, hoping I'll miss my train. I won't.

THAW. So nothing I've said—what little I've had a chance to say . . . (*She shakes her head.*)—you still intend to divorce me?

NORA. Oh, I never said I was divorcing you. I'm deserting you. So you can divorce me.

THAW. You do realize, Nora, that if a wife deserts her husband he doesn't have to pay her alimony?

NORA. I don't want alimony. But I do want severance pay. (*Points to books.*) There's my bill, rendered for 10 years of domestic services—the thing sticking in *Woman's Place,* by Cynthia Fuchs Epstein. I figured it at the going agency rates for a full-time cook, cleaning woman, handyman, laundress, seamstress, and part-time gardener and chauffeur. I've worked an average ten-hour day. So I've charged for overtime. Of course, you've paid my rent, taxes, clothing, medical expenses and food. So I've deducted those. Even though as a housewife, I've had no fringe benefits. Just the same, the bill . . . well, I'm afraid you're going to be staggered. I was. It comes to over $53,000. I'd like to be paid in 10 installments.

THAW. (*He is staggered.*) Mathematics isn't really your bag, Nora.

NORA. I did it on that little calculating machine you gave me at Christmas. If you think it's not really fair, I'll be glad to negotiate. And, please notice, I haven't charged anything for sleeping with you!

THAW. Wow! (*He is really punch drunk.*)

NORA. I'm not a prostitute. And *this* is what I wanted to say about the Lib girls. They're right about women who marry *just* for money. But they're wrong about women who marry for love. It's love makes all the difference—

THAW. (*Dispirited.*) Well, *vive la différence.*

NORA. And, of course, I haven't charged anything for being a nurse. I've adored taking care of the children, especially when they were babies. I'm going to miss them—*awfully.*

THAW. (*On his feet, with outrage.*) You're deserting the children, too? My God, Nora, what kind of woman *are* you? You're going to leave those poor little kids alone in this house—

NORA. You're here. And I told you, your mother is coming. I wired her that her son needed her. She'll be happy again—and be needed again—for the first time in years—

THAW. (*This is a real blow*) My *mother!* Oh migod you *can't,* Nora. You know how she—*swarms* over me! She thinks I'm still 12 years old . . . (*His head is now in his hands.*) You know she drives me out of my cotton-picking mind.

NORA. Yes. But you never said so before.

THAW. I love my mother. She's been a good mother, and wife. But, Nora, she's a *very* limited woman! Yak, yak—food, shopping, the kids . . .

NORA. Thaw, the children love this house, and I don't want to take them out of school. And I can't give them another home. Women, you know, can't borrow money to buy a house. Besides, legally this house and everything in it, except my mother's few things and my wedding presents, are yours. All the worldly goods with which thou didst me endow seem to be in that suitcase.

THAW. Nora, you know damn well that all my life insurance is in your name. If I died tomorrow—and I'll probably blow my brains out tonight—everything would go to you and the kids.

NORA. Widowhood is one of the few fringe benefits of marriage. But, today, all the money I have is what I've saved in the past year out of my clothes allowance—$260.33. But I hope you will give me my severance pay—

THAW. And if I don't—you know legally I don't have to—how do you propose to support yourself?

NORA. Well, if I can't get a job right away—sell my engagement ring. That's why they say diamonds are a gal's best friend. What else do most women *have* they can turn into ready cash—except their bodies?

THAW. What kind of job do you figure on getting?

NORA. Well, I do have a master's in English. So I'm going to try for a spot in TIME Research. That's the intellectual harem kept by the Time Inc. editors. The starting pay is good.

THAW. How do you know that?

NORA. From your own research assistant, Molly Peapack. We're both Wellesley, you know. She's a friend of the chief researcher at TIME, Marylois Vega. Also, Molly says, computer programming is a field that may open to women—

THAW. (*Indignant.*) You told Peapack you were leaving me? Before you even told *me*? How do you like *that* for treating a mate like an inferior!

NORA. Thaw, I've told you at least three times a week for the last year that with the kids both in school, I'd like to get a job. You always laughed at me. You said I was too old to be a Playboy Bunny, and that the only job an inexperienced woman my age could get would be as a saleswoman—

THAW. Okay. Where are you going to live?

NORA. Peapack's offered to let me stay with her until I find something—

THAW. I'm going to have a word with Miss Molly Peapack tomorrow. She's been too damned aggressive lately, anyway—

NORA. She's going to have a word with you, too. *She's* leaving.

THAW. Peapack is leaving? Leaving *me*?

NORA. When you got her from Prudential, you promised her, remember, you'd recommend her for promotion to office manager. So, last week you took on a man. A new man. Now she's got a job offer where she's sure she's got a 40–60 chance for advancement to management. So you've lost your home wife and your office wife, too.

THAW. And *this* is a male-dominated world?

NORA. Thaw, I've got just five minutes—

THAW. You've still not told me *why*—

NORA. Oh, Thaw darling! You poor—*man*. I have told you why: I'm leaving because I want a job. I want to do some share, however small, of the world's work, and be paid for it. Isn't the work you do in the world—and the salary *you* get—what makes you respect yourself, and other men respect *you*? Women have begun to want to respect themselves a little, too—

THAW. You mean, the real reason you are leaving is that you want a *paying* job?

NORA. Yes.

THAW. God, Nora, why didn't you say that in the beginning? All right, go get a job, if it's that important to you. But that doesn't mean you have to leave me and the kids.

NORA. I'm afraid it does. Otherwise, I'd have to do two jobs. Out there. And here.

THAW. Look, Nora, I heard some of the Lib gals say there are millions of working wives and mothers who are doing two jobs. Housework can't be all that rough—

NORA. Scrubbing floors, walls. Cleaning pots, pans, windows, ovens. Messes—dog messes, toilet messes, children's messes. Garbage. Laundry. Shopping for pounds of stuff. Loading them into the car, out of the car—(*A pause.*) Not all of it hard. But all of it routine. All of it *boring.*

THAW. Listen, Nora, what say, you work, I work. And we split the housework? How's that for a deal?

NORA. It's a deal you are not quite free to make, Thaw. You sometimes *can't* get home until very late. And you have to travel a lot, you know. Oh, it might work for a little while. But not for long. After 10 years, you still won't empty an ashtray, or pick up after yourself in the bathroom. No. I don't have the physical or moral strength to swing two jobs. So I've got to choose the one, before it's too late, that's most important for me—oh, not for me just now, but for when *I'm* 50—

THAW. When you're 50, Nora, if you don't leave me, you'll be the wife of the president of Stone Mountain Life Insurance Company. Sharing my wealth, sharing whatever status I have in the community. And with servants of your own. Now you listen to *me,* Nora. It's a man's world, out there. It's a man's world where there are a lot of women working. I see them every day. What are most of them really doing? Marking time, and looking, always looking, for a man who will offer them a woman's world . . . the world you have here. Marriage is still the best deal that the world has to offer women. And most women know it. It's always been like that. And it's going to be like that for a long, long time.

NORA. Just now I feel that the best deal I, Nora Wald, can hope to get out of life is to learn to esteem myself as a person . . . to stop feeling that every day a little bit more of my mind—and heart—is being washed down the drain with the soapsuds. . . . Thaw—listen. If I don't stop shrinking, I'll end up secretly hating you, and trying to cut you—and *your* son—down to my size. The way your swarmy mommie does you and your Dad. And you'll become like your father, the typical henpecked husband. Thinking of his old wife as the Ball and Chain. You know he has a mistress? (*Thaw knows. He belts down a stiff drink.*) A smart gal who owns her own shop . . . a woman who doesn't bore him.

THAW. Well, Nora . . . (*Pours another drink.*) One for the road?

NORA. Right. For the road.

THAW. Nora . . . I'll wait. But I don't know how long—

NORA. I've thought of that, too . . . that you might remarry . . . that girl, maybe, who means nothing—

THAW. Dammit, a man needs a woman of his own—

NORA. (*Nodding.*) I know. A sleep-in, sleep-with body servant of his very own. Well, that's your problem. Just now, I have to wrestle with my problem . . . (*Goes to door, picks up suitcase.*) I'm not bursting with self-confidence, Thaw. I do love you. And I also need . . . a man. So I'm not slamming the door. I'm closing it . . . very . . . softly.

(*Exits. Curtain falls.*)

yin		yang
female		male
dark,		light
passive		active
receptive		generative
negative		positive
cold		hot
wet		dry
weak		strong

*The **yin** and **yang**, symbols from Chinese philosophy, represent a universe of dynamic forces, always changing but well ordered and governed by laws in which both contradiction and harmony exist and both unity and multiplicity prevail.*

Questions

1.   According to critics, those active in the woman's movement are almost exclusively members of the white upper-middle class; blacks have been conspicuously absent from feminist activities. If such a charge is true, why has Luce included a black as one of four feminist participants on a television show perceived only in its audial dimension by the audience?

2.   Do both Thaw and Nora show a believable range of human strengths and weaknesses, or are they one-dimensional or "straw-man" characters? Is the writer more concerned with character or with idea?

3.   Does the play try to make you "think" or "believe"? Is the dominant appeal emotional or logical? Predict how various categories of people would respond to the play. Has the writer deliberately aimed for a particular type of audience?

4.   Is such a drama an effective way of presenting a problem? Are Thaw and Nora a "typical" American couple in terms of their

marriage? Their economic situation? Their race? Their political orientation? Their values?

5. If this play articulates with reasonable accuracy the state of many American marriages, how do you suppose such a state came about? Does society have any structures which force a woman to follow certain paths? If so, are the structures institutionalized or simply passed from mother to daughter? Do you expect to have the kind of marriage that Thaw and Nora have? If so, what do you expect to gain from such a relationship? If not, how will you avoid their type of marriage?

6. Try your hand at writing a short drama showing how "male chauvinism" operates in a dating relationship or how it is the woman who already dominates the man in our society.

Below is a cross cultural test; in seventeen out of eighteen cultures tested, women prefer the figures on the left and men those on the right. Describe the difference between the male and female styles.

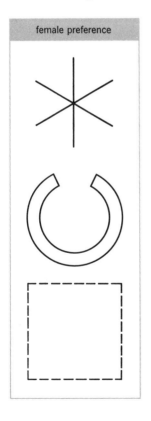

female preference

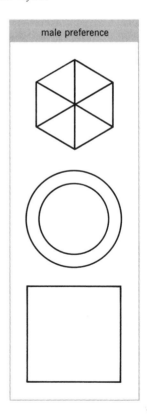

male preference

The Problem
That Has No Name

BETTY FRIEDAN

The problem lay buried, unspoken, for many years in the minds of American women. It was a strange stirring, a sense of dissatisfaction, a yearning that women suffered in the middle of the twentieth century in the United States. Each suburban wife struggled with it alone. As she made the beds, shopped for groceries, matched slipcover material, ate peanut butter sandwiches with her children, chauffeured Cub Scouts and Brownies, lay beside her husband at night—she was afraid to ask even of herself the silent question—"Is this all?"

For over fifteen years there was no word of this yearning in the millions of words written about women, for women, in all the columns, books and articles by experts telling women their role was to seek fulfillment as wives and mothers. Over and over women heard in voices of tradition and of Freudian sophistication that they could desire no greater destiny than to glory in their own femininity. Experts told them how to catch a man and keep him, how to breastfeed children and handle their toilet training, how to cope with sibling rivalry and adolescent rebellion; how to buy a dishwasher, bake bread, cook gourmet snails, and build a swimming pool with their own hands; how to dress, look, and act more feminine and make marriage more exciting; how to keep their husbands from dying

Reprinted from *The Feminine Mystique* by Betty Friedan. By permission of W.W. Norton & Company, Inc. Copyright © 1963 by Betty Friedan.

young and their sons from growing into delinquents. They were taught to pity the neurotic, unfeminine, unhappy women who wanted to be poets or physicists or presidents. They learned that truly feminine women do not want careers, higher education, political rights— the independence and the opportunities that the old-fashioned feminists fought for. Some women, in their forties and fifties, still remembered painfully giving up those dreams, but most of the younger women no longer even thought about them. A thousand expert voices applauded their femininity, their adjustment, their new maturity. All they had to do was devote their lives from earliest girlhood to finding a husband and bearing children.

By the end of the nineteen-fifties, the average marriage age of women in America dropped to 20, and was still dropping, into the teens. Fourteen million girls were engaged by 17. The proportion of women attending college in comparison with men dropped from 47 per cent in 1920 to 35 per cent in 1958. A century earlier, women had fought for higher education; now girls went to college to get a husband. By the mid-fifties, 60 per cent dropped out of college to marry, or because they were afraid too much education would be a marriage bar. Colleges built dormitories for "married students," but the students were almost always the husbands. A new degree was instituted for the wives—"Ph.T." (Putting Husband Through).

Then American girls began getting married in high school. And the women's magazines, deploring the unhappy statistics about these young marriages, urged that courses on marriage, and marriage counselors, be installed in the high schools. Girls started going steady at twelve and thirteen, in junior high. Manufacturers put out brassiers with false bosoms of foam rubber for little girls of ten. And an advertisement for a child's dress, sizes 3–6x, in the *New York Times* in the fall of 1960, said: "She Too Can Join the Man-Trap Set."

By the end of the fifties, the United States birthrate was overtaking India's. The birth-control movement, renamed Planned Parenthood, was asked to find a method whereby women who had been advised that a third or fourth baby would be born dead or defective might have it anyhow. Statisticians were especially astounded at the fantastic increase in the number of babies among college women. Where once they had two children, now they had four, five, six. Women who had once wanted careers were now making careers out of having babies. So rejoiced *Life* magazine in a 1956 paean to the movement of American women back to the home.

In a New York hospital, a woman had a nervous breakdown when she found she could not breastfeed her baby. In other hospitals, women dying of cancer refused a drug which research had proved might save their lives: its side effects were said to be unfeminine. "If I have only one life, let me live it as a blonde," a larger-than-life-sized picture of a pretty, vacuous woman proclaimed from newspaper, magazine, and drugstore ads. And across America, three out of every ten women dyed their hair blonde. They ate a chalk called Metrecal, instead of food, to shrink to the size of the thin young models. Department-store buyers reported that American women, since 1939, had become three and four sizes smaller. "Women are out to fit the clothes, instead of vice-versa," one buyer said.

Interior decorators were designing kitchens with mosaic murals and original paintings, for kitchens were once again the center of women's lives. Home sewing became a million-dollar industry. Many women no longer left their homes, except to shop, chauffeur their children, or attend a social engagement with their husbands. Girls were growing up in America without ever having jobs outside the home. In the late fifties, a sociological phenomenon was suddenly remarked: a third of American women now worked, but most were no longer young and very few were pursuing careers. They were married women who held part-time jobs, selling or secretarial, to put their husbands through school, their sons through college, or to help pay the mortgage. Or they were widows supporting families. Fewer and fewer women were entering professional work. The shortages in the nursing, social work, and teaching professions caused crises in almost every American city. Concerned over the Soviet Union's lead in the space race, scientists noted that America's greatest source of unused brain-power was women. But girls would not study physics: it was "unfeminine." A girl refused a science fellowship at Johns Hopkins to take a job in a real-estate office. All she wanted, she said, was what every other American girl wanted—to get married, have four children and live in a nice house in a nice suburb.

The suburban housewife—she was the dream image of the young American women and the envy, it was said, of women all over the world. The American housewife—freed by science and labor-saving appliances from the drudgery, the dangers of childbirth and the illnesses of her grandmother. She was healthy, beautiful, educated, concerned only about her husband, her children, her home. She had found true feminine fulfillment. As a housewife and mother, she was respected as a full and equal partner to man in his world. She was free to choose automobiles, clothes, appliances, supermarkets; she had everything that women ever dreamed of.

In the fifteen years after World War II, this mystique of feminine fulfillment became the cherished and self-perpetuating core of contemporary American culture. Millions of women lived their lives in the image of those pretty pictures of the American suburban housewife, kissing their husbands goodbye in front of the picture window, depositing their stationwagonsful of children at school, and smiling as they ran the new electric waxer over the spotless kitchen floor. They baked their own bread, sewed their own and their children's clothes, kept their new washing machines and dryers running all day. They changed the sheets on the beds twice a week instead of once, took the rug-hooking class in adult education, and pitied their poor frustrated mothers, who had dreamed of having a career. Their only dream was to be perfect wives and mothers; their highest ambition to have five children and a beautiful house, their only fight to get and keep their husbands. They had no thought for the unfeminine problems of the world outside the home; they wanted the men to make the major decisions. They gloried in their role as women, and wrote proudly on the census blank: "Occupation: housewife."

For over fifteen years, the words written for women, and the words women used when they talked to each other, while their husbands sat on the other side of the room and talked shop or politics or septic tanks, were about problems with their children, or how to keep their husbands happy, or improve their children's school, or cook chicken or make slipcovers. Nobody argued whether women were inferior or superior to men; they were simply different. Words like "emancipation" and "career" sounded strange and embarrassing; no one had used them for years. When a Frenchwoman named Simone de Beauvoir wrote a book called *The Second Sex*, an American critic commented that she obviously "didn't know what life was all about," and besides, she was talking about French women. The "woman problem" in America no longer existed.

If a woman had a problem in the 1950's and 1960's, she knew that something must be wrong with her marriage, or with herself. Other women were satisfied with their lives, she thought. What kind of a woman was she if she did not feel this mysterious fulfillment waxing the kitchen floor? She was so ashamed to admit her dissatisfaction that she never knew how many other women shared it. If she tried to tell her husband, he didn't understand what she was talking about. She did not really understand it herself. For over fifteen years women in America found it harder to talk about this problem than about sex. Even the psychoanalysts had no name for it. When a woman went to a psychiatrist for help, as many women did, she would say, "I'm so ashamed," or "I must be hopelessly neurotic." "I don't know what's wrong with women today," a suburban psychiatrist said uneasily. "I only know something is wrong because most of my patients happen to be women. And their problem isn't sexual." Most women with this problem did not go to see a psychoanalyst, however. "There's nothing wrong really," they kept telling themselves. "There isn't any problem."

But on an April morning in 1959, I heard a mother of four, having coffee with four other mothers in a suburban development fifteen miles from New York, say in a tone of quiet desperation, "the problem." And the others knew, without words, that she was not talking about a problem with her husband, or her children, or her home. Suddenly they realized they all shared the same problem, the problem that has no name. They began, hesitantly, to talk about it. Later, after they had picked up their children at nursery school and taken them home to nap, two of the women cried, in sheer relief, just to know they were not alone.

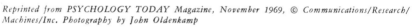

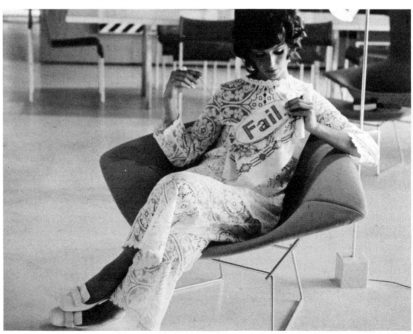

Questions

1.   Is the question "Is this all?" something women ask while men have an answer? If so, why is the problem almost exclusively that of women? If not, can the whole question even be considered in "female" (rather than societal) terms? (For an in-depth investigation of the question "Is this all?" see the book of *Ecclesiastes* in the Bible.)

2.   Do you suppose that *each* suburban housewife actually struggles with the same problem and has the same responses? If not, why does Friedan speak of the suburban housewife in such comprehensive terms? Is the percentage of women sharing the same problem important? Why suburban rather than urban?

3.   How does the author make her case convincing? Who is she trying to convince?

4.   What part do you suppose advertising has played in creating "the problem"? What is the "feminine mystique"? How has it been perpetuated?

5.   In concluding her book, Friedan explains what a woman must do to find salvation:

The only way for a woman, as for a man, to find herself, to know herself as a person, is by creative work of her own. There is no other way. But a job, any job, is not the answer—in fact, it can be part of the trap. Women who do not look for jobs equal to their actual capacity, who do not let themselves develop the lifetime interests and goals which require serious education and training, who take a job at twenty or forty to "help out at home" or just to kill extra time, are walking, almost as surely as the ones who stay inside the housewife trap, to a nonexistent future.

Is such a solution applicable to 51% of our population? Does Friedan mean it to be? Is her solution a worthwhile ideal? A realistic ideal? Are those with "creative work" necessarily happier than others? More fulfilled?

6.   Write the dialogue and explain the actions for a short sketch in which you demonstrate "the problem that has no name." Which is more necessary to communicate the ideas of the sketch: words or actions?

Dear Mrs. Friedan

MARGARET BENNETT

Dear Mrs. Friedan,

Just a few short years ago—before I read your book—I was what you describe as an average, intelligent, upper-middle-class housewife in her thirties with a successful professional man husband, four lovely children, and a split-level home on a pseudo-rural road in a fashionable suburb. I was spending my time doing all those normal little humdrum things that, as you reported, an average, intelligent, upper-middle-class housewife in her thirties with a successful professional man husband, four lovely children, and a split-level home on a pseudo-rural road in a fashionable suburb does. You know, things like becoming an alcoholic, having affairs with door-to-door salesmen, turning my sons into homosexuals, pushing my teen-age daughter into sexual promiscuity, castrating my husband, running shrieking through the streets at night without my clothes on, and making almost daily attempts at suicide. But even though I kept frantically busy doing these things which by all rights *ought* to make a woman feel alive, I still had that vague sense of dissatisfaction. I felt empty and somehow incomplete. I kept asking myself, is this all there is?

But I had no answer, and no one else had an answer *for* me,

From the Book *Alice in Womanland* by Margaret Bennett. © 1967 by June Biermann and Barbara Toohey. Published by Prentice-Hall, Inc., Englewood Cliffs, New Jersey.

either—not my gynecologist, not my obstetrician, not my internist, not my psychiatrist, not my dermatologist, not my optometrist, not my chiropodist, not my manicurist. They kept telling me there was nothing really wrong with me. So I'd just go home and take another handful of tranquilizers or have another baby or a hysterectomy or run off to Acapulco and shack up with a beach boy for a while. But none of these typical American housewives' solutions seemed to help me, either.

Then one day it happened. As usual, I had forgotten to send the Literary Guild card back, and your book arrived. Since I used to waste a good percentage of my time, as you put it, "reading books nobody talks about," I plunged right in. I hadn't gone through five pages before I realized it was ME you were writing about, ME, the average, intelligent, upper-middle-class housewife in her thirties with a successful professional man husband, four lovely children, and a split-level home on a pseudo-rural road in a fashionable suburb. ME. I had the problem that had no name. I had the hunger that food cannot sate. I had the thirst that martinis cannot quench. I had the desire that multiple orgasms cannot satisfy. I had the itch that long, well-manicured fingernails cannot scratch. And by the time my trembling hands closed your book, I knew you had the answer I was looking for. It was all so beautifully simple.

In order to salvage my life and keep from destroying my husband and children, I had to take my place in the SALT MINES, for that was where I really belonged.

As I looked back over my life, I remembered that from my earliest years I had longed to be a salt miner. At first, my parents had laughed indulgently and taken my ambition with a grain of salt. But when I became a teen-ager and still remained steadfast in my career decision, they began to worry about me, especially mother with her rigid preconception of the feminine role. I remember her saying to me over and over again, "Nancy, wanting to be a salt miner is . . . well . . . peculiar for a girl. It's unfeminine. Salt mining is a man's job. And, anyway, you're going to grow up to be an average, intelligent, upper-middle-class housewife with a successful professional man husband, four lovely children, and a split-level home on a pseudo-rural road in a fashionable suburb, so you might as well give up this silly idea about salt mining once and for all."

But I didn't give it up. After high school, defying my parents who had enrolled me in Miss Frobisher's finishing school, I ran away to Texas. To support myself I got a part-time job as a miner's lampwick trimmer, happy to do the humblest task just to be associated with salt mining. At the same time I entered Texas A & M to study mining engineering. I showed such promise that at the end of my freshman year, I was awarded a full scholarship to continue my studies.

But then a shadow fell across my joy—a tall, square-shouldered shadow, John's shadow. John was majoring in accounting with the idea of going on to law school. "Nothing can come of this between us," he told me one afternoon as we strolled hand-in-hand through the mesquite. "I'm only going to be a wealthy, successful tax attorney. How can the life I have to offer you compete with the lure of the salt mines?"

That started me thinking about the cold, lonely isolation of a career in the mines. All spring I grew more worried and disturbed as I thought about my future and watched all my friends get married. Finally, I knew I had to decide one way or the other. The dictates of the feminine mystique tipped the balance. I gave up the scholarship with a kind of relief and enrolled instead in a Texas junior college which was famous for its curriculum in baton twirling. I graduated from there cum laude and married John. For years afterwards I skirted the colorful salt box displays in supermarkets and I couldn't bear to keep a salt cellar on my table. It was too painful. I couldn't even attend homemade ice cream parties, because the laughing faces around the freezer twirling in the ice and rock salt seemed to mock my lost ambition.

And, but for your book, I might have gone on like this forever, suffering a slow death of mind and spirit, confined to my comfortable concentration camp, denying my dream. But your words gave me the courage to become more than John's wife, or Terry, Mark, Allan, and Betsy's mother, or the PTA's refreshment committee chairman or the Fuller Brush Man's mistress. You inspired me to find personal identity as a capable, vital, respected salt miner.

Oh, I won't pretend it was easy at first. John and the children were violently opposed, because they had the silly notion that my eight hours on the job and half-hour each way going to and from work and an occasional overtime weekend and the three nights a week I spent in mining engineering class would be hours taken away from them. In the beginning, I'll admit I also found it a little difficult adjusting to getting up at four-thirty in the morning to do my housework before going off to the mines.

Then, there were some small difficulties on the job, too. I found the other miners, all of whom were men, resented me. They felt I was one of those foolish, dilettantish dabblers seeking self-enrichment in salt mining instead of a person with a serious commitment. I managed to win their respect, however, by showing my willingness to start at the bottom, crawling around on my hands and knees down in the deepest, narrowest, most winding passages. And now I've reached the point where they let me stand on my own two feet and work in the higher tunnels, stretching myself to the fullest.

But it's not just the professional success and status I've gained from my new career, not just the glorious feeling that I'm doing work that contributes to the human community—it's the change that's come over my total being. Where once I lived in that terrible monotony, unpunctuated with triumph or disaster that you mention, now my life teems with cave-ins, fire-damp explosions, gas seepages, rock slides, all those crises that keep boredom on the run and give life its savor. Now I have that glorious anxiety that comes with freedom. While before I was occasionally a victim of that inexplicable tiredness you call "housewife's fatigue," now every night I experience the straight-forward, total exhaustion of a person who has spent eight hours in the salt mine. No longer do I pester my doctors with vague, undiagnosable complaints, either. Now I present them with concrete cases of ruptured intervertebral discs, emphysema, and hemorrhaging ulcers.

My commitment to the salt mines has made a big difference for my family, too. I never scream at my children or nag my husband the way I used to. In fact, I hardly ever even see them. Left to their own devices, my sons have made dramatic gains in virile independence. Only last week, all by themselves, they mixed up their own little Molotov cocktail and blew the rear end out of the garage. My formerly shy daughter, too, seems to be blossoming in her new-found freedom. She no longer needs the slightest push from me into promiscuity. And from all reports, my husband, as a result of my extended periods of absence from home, has begun to reach startling heights of potency.

Of course, it's also true that I do have to cope with the hostility of the other housewives who have not had the courage to say no to the "mystique." At social gatherings when they hear me rave on about my days in the salt mines, their eyes fill with envious hatred. They silently compare their own existence with mine—their depressing, endless hours of doing whatever they feel like doing whenever they feel like doing it, their days destroyed in dehumanizing activities like baking brioches or playing golf or bridge or meeting their husbands downtown for lunch or visiting an art gallery or seeing a play or taking the kids to the zoo or attending a course in conversational French or space-age astronomy or Great Books.

Yes, when I contrast this with the way my days are spent in the salt mines, I begin to fully realize what you have done for me. You have delivered me from the problem that has no name. Of course, I still have problems—more than I could ever have imagined possible—but I assure you, EVERY SINGLE ONE OF THEM HAS A NAME.

And so I thank you, Betty Friedan, and I urge you to keep helping each average, intelligent, upper-middle-class housewife in her thirties with a successful professional man husband, four lovely children, and a split-level home on a pseudo-rural road in a fashionable suburb to find her own personal salt mine—some deep commitment which can totally swallow up her life. For only in that way can you deliver her from the chilling climate of unexpectation and give her what you have given me, something at last to look forward to in life: retirement.

Sincerely yours,

Questions

1.   Is the letter format an effective way to respond to Betty Friedan's ideas? (This letter originally appeared as a segment of a chapter of a book.) Are both authors writing for similar audiences?

2.   What role does the writer adopt? Why? How does the writer poke fun at Betty Friedan?

3.   What use is made of repetition? Why?

4.   Is humor an effective way to answer a serious book like *The Feminine Mystique*? An honest way?

The Feminine Mistaque

ART BUCHWALD

Unlike most American husbands, I am very concerned about the problems of the modern American Woman and her struggle for fulfillment. My bible has been *The Feminine Mystique,* and no one admires Betty Friedan, the author, more than I do.

Therefore, the other night when I came home from work and found my wife scrubbing the floor, I said to her, "Do you know who you are?"

"I'm sorry," she said blankly. "What did you say?"

"Do you know who you are? Do you have any identity besides being a wife, a mother and a servant?"

"I don't think so," she replied. "Don't step over there. I just mopped it."

"Aren't you concerned that you've traded in your brains for a broom? Can you stand there and tell me that you are contented, happy and satisfied with your lot?"

"Would you rinse out this pail for me?" she said. "I want to know one thing. Are you trying to start a fight with me, are you trying out a new article idea on me, or are you trying to cover up something that you've done?"

"I'm not doing any of them. But I happened to have read *The*

Feminine Mystique, and it occurs to me you should want more out of life than this drab existence that you're leading now."

"I'm baking some homemade bread," she said. "I hope the kids like it."

"Answer my question."

"Well, if you must know, I would really like to be a mailman, but I'm afraid to take the civil-service exam."

"That's right, make fun of me. All over America there are millions of unhappy, unfulfilled women who are searching for a place in the sun, who are nothing but sex objects to their husbands, and you stand there making bread and then tell me you're satisfied."

"I didn't say I was satisfied," she said, "but I figure I've got a pretty good deal and I don't want to louse it up."

"You know why you don't want to louse it up?" I said to her as she set the table for dinner. "Because you're dominated by me. I've denied you your birthright and destroyed you as an individual."

"Maybe I could join a sit-in at the White House."

"That's not what I'm talking about. By being a mother and a wife you are suffering from a problem that has no name. You are lavishing love and affection on me and the children, and this is causing havoc to your id."

"Now don't start knocking my id," she said, draining the spaghetti into a pan. "I know I look out for you and I take care of the children and I keep the house clean and I entertain well—but nobody's perfect."

She then asked me to make her a drink.

"Ah-hah," I said. "Do you know there are a million known alcoholic housewives in this country and there are another million who are on tranquilizers? Why is that?"

"I have no idea."

"Because they are unfulfilled. They are searching for something they'll never find in their homes."

"Maybe I'll go out and have an affair."

"You don't have to go that far," I told her.

"How far do you want me to go?"

"Outside this house is a whole new world. Go out and embrace it. Find the *real* you."

"I will if you go find the children. Dinner is ready."

Later that night, as she was putting up her hair, I noticed she yawned.

"Why did you yawn?" I asked her.

"I'm tired."

"No you're not, you're suffering from housewives' fatigue," I said triumphantly. "Betty Friedan calls it 'the illness that has no name.' No doctor can get at its cause or cure. You are slowly dying of boredom. Every intelligent, able-bodied woman who has no goal, no ambition to make her stretch and grow, is committing a kind of suicide. Do you think I want to live with that on my conscience the rest of my life?"

"Do you mean to say, every time I yawn, you feel guilty?"

"Something like that," I admitted.

"OK, if you want me to take my rightful place in society, I will."

A few nights later I came home from work, and found the front door wide open, the kids in the kitchen eating corn flakes, the dog tearing up the rug and the television set going full blast.

"Where's your mother?" I asked.

"She said to tell you she got a job with Sears, Roebuck and she has to work until nine tonight," my 10-year-old said as she took a swing at her brother.

It took me 20 minutes to get her on the phone. "You come home right away," I shouted. "Do you realize what is going on around here?"

"I'll be home at nine. I've finally found myself. The real me."

"Where?"

"Between the pot-holder counter and ladies' pajamas. Now I know what it is to be fulfilled."

I walked into the kitchen, and my son said, "You want puffed wheat or corn flakes?"

"Corn flakes," I said sadly. "Go easy on the milk."

Questions

1. What is the effect of Buchwald's use of dialogue?

2. What persona does Buchwald adopt? Why?

3. What is the effect of the husband telling his wife that she should be liberated?

4. What point does Buchwald make about what happens when we try to interpret the actions of others? Can everyday habits reasonably be interpreted in terms of an ideological framework?

5. The title of this volume uses the word "identity" in relation to male and female. Do you think an awareness of one's male or female identity is important? Does it make a difference what sort of conditions are associated with our identity?

6. Should a person hold firmly to a certain knowledge of his identity (as Buchwald's wife does at first) or try to find his or her "real" worth and meaning through a philosophical or moral construct? That is, which is most important: who you are or who you might become? Is psychological stability more likely to be associated with one than the other? Are these mutually exclusive alternatives?

Seneca Falls Declaration

ELIZABETH CADY STANTON

The history of mankind is a history of repeated injuries and usurpations on the part of man toward woman, having in direct object the establishment of an absolute tyranny over her. To prove this, let facts be submitted to a candid world.

He has never permitted her to exercise her inalienable right to the elective franchise.

He has compelled her to submit to laws, in the formation of which she had no voice.

He has withheld from her rights which are given to the most ignorant and degraded men—both natives and foreigners.

Having deprived her of this first right of a citizen, the elective franchise, thereby leaving her without representation in the halls of legislation, he has oppressed her on all sides.

He has made her, if married, in the eye of the law, civilly dead.

He has taken from her all right in property, even to the wages she earns.

He has made her, morally, an irresponsible being, as she can commit many crimes with impunity, provided they be done in the presence of her husband. In the covenant of marriage, she is compelled to promise obedience to her husband, he becoming, to all intents and purposes, her master—the law giving him power to deprive her of her liberty, and to administer chastisement.

He has so framed the law of divorce, as to what shall be the proper causes, and in case of separation, to whom the guardianship of the children shall be given, as to be wholly regardless of the happiness of women—the law, in all cases, going upon a false supposition of the supremacy of man, and giving all power into his hands.

After depriving her of all rights as a married woman, if single, and the owner of property, he has taxed her to support a government which recognizes her only when her property can be made profitable to it.

He has monopolized nearly all the profitable employments, and from those she is permitted to follow, she receives but a scanty remuneration. He closes against her all the avenues to wealth and distinction which he considers most honorable to himself. As a teacher of theology, medicine, or law, she is not known.

He has denied her the facilities for obtaining a thorough education, all colleges being closed against her.

He allows her in Church, as well as State, but a subordinate position, claiming Apostolic authority for her exclusion from the ministry, and, with some exceptions, from any participation in the affairs of the Church.

He has created a false public sentiment by giving to the world a different code of morals for men and women, by which moral delinquencies which exclude women from society, are not only tolerated, but deemed of little account in man.

He has usurped the prerogative of Jehovah himself, claiming it as his right to assign for her a sphere of action, when that belongs to her conscience and to her God.

He has endeavored in every way that he could, to destroy her confidence in her own powers, to lessen her self-respect, and to make her willing to lead a dependent and abject life.

Questions

1.   Elizabeth Cady Stanton wrote this document in 1848 at the Woman's Rights Convention in Seneca Falls, New York. What changes in the status of women have occurred in the last century and a quarter? Is the condition of women better for these changes? Of men? Of children? Of the family? Of society?

2.   The form of the Declaration supposedly came as a flash of inspiration to the author on the eve of the convention. Is following the recital of wrongs in the Declaration of Independence an effective rhetorical technique? To whom would it appeal most?

3.   "Man" is considered in general and inclusive terms; if the statements of this declaration contain any truth about "man's" conspiracy to prevent woman from securing her rights, how and why were women granted the requests of this century-old document? Could a majority of the men have supported any of the things all are accused of supporting?

Sexual Politics:
A Manifesto for Revolution

KATE MILLET

When one group rules another, the relationship between the two is political. When such an arrangement is carried out over a long period of time it develops an ideology (feudalism, racism, etc.). All historical civilizations are patriarchies: their ideology is male supremacy.

Oppressed groups are denied education, economic independence, the power of office, representation, an image of dignity and self-respect, equality of status, and recognition as human beings. Throughout history women have been consistently denied all of these, and their denial today, while attenuated and partial, is nevertheless consistent. The education allowed them is deliberately designed to be inferior, and they are systematically programmed out of and excluded from the knowledge where power lies today—e.g., in science and technology. They are confined to conditions of economic dependence based on the sale of their sexuality in marriage, or a variety of prostitutions. Work on a basis of economic independence allows them only a subsistence level of life—often not even that. They do not hold office, are represented in no positions of power, and authority is forbidden them. The image of woman fostered by cultural media, high and low, then and now, is a marginal and demeaning existence, and one outside the human condition—which is defined as the prerogative of man, the male.

Government is upheld by power, which is supported through consent (social opinion), or imposed by violence. Conditioning to an ideology amounts to the former. But there may be a resort to the latter at any moment when consent is withdrawn—rape, attack, sequestration, beatings, murder. Sexual politics obtains consent through the "socialization" of both sexes to patriarchal policies. They consist of the following:

1) the formation of human personality along stereotyped lines of sexual category, based on the needs and values of the master class and dictated by what he would cherish in himself and find convenient in an underclass: aggression, intellectuality, force and efficiency for the male; passivity, ignorance, docility, "virtue," and ineffectuality for the female.

2) the concept of sex role, which assigns domestic service and attendance upon infants to all females and the rest of human interest, achievement and ambition to the male; the charge of leader at all times and places to the male, and the duty of follower, with equal uniformity, to the female.

3) the imposition of male rule through institutions: patriarchal religion, the proprietary family, marriage, "The Home," masculine oriented culture, and a pervasive doctrine of male superiority.

A Sexual Revolution would bring about the following conditions, desirable upon rational, moral and humanistic grounds:

1) the end of sexual repression—freedom of expression and of sexual mores (sexual freedom has been partially attained, but it is now being subverted beyond freedom into exploitative license for patriarchal and reactionary ends).

2) Unisex, or the end of separatist character-structure, temperament and behavior, so that each individual may develop an entire —rather than a partial, limited, and conformist—personality.

3) re-examination of traits categorized into "masculine" and "feminine," with a total reassessment as to their human usefulness and advisability in both sexes. Thus if "masculine" violence is undesirable, it is so for both sexes, "feminine" dumb-cow passivity likewise. If "masculine" intelligence or efficiency is valuable, it is so for both sexes equally, and the same must be true for "feminine" tenderness or consideration.

4) the end of sex role and sex status, the patriarchy and the male supremacist ethic, attitude and ideology—in all areas of endeavor, experience, and behavior.

5) the end of the ancient oppression of the young under the

patriarchal proprietary family, their chattel status, the attainment of the human rights presently denied them, the professionalization and therefore improvement of their care, and the guarantee that when they enter the world, they are desired, planned for, and provided with equal opportunities.

6) Bisex, or the end of enforced perverse heterosexuality, so that the sex act ceases to be arbitrarily polarized into male and female, to the exclusion of sexual expression between members of the same sex.

7) the end of sexuality in the forms in which it has existed historically—brutality, violence, capitalism, exploitation, and warfare—that it may cease to be hatred and become love.

8) the attainment of the female sex to freedom and full human status after millennia of deprivation and oppression, and of both sexes to a viable humanity.

Questions

1.   Carefully examine the opening paragraph. What is a "group"? Do all females constitute a single "group"? All males? What does it mean to "rule"? Can the male–female relationship be called "political," or is Millet's connection of sex with politics primarily rhetorical in purpose?

2.   Kate Millet is a professor who has taught at such colleges as Barnard & Bryn Mawr. Does her education and position contradict her argument that women consistently have been "denied education, economic independence, the power of office, representation, an image of dignity and self-respect, equality of status, and recognition as human beings"? How would she answer this charge? Is it fair to ask if the author's own position contradicts her assertions?

3.   Is marriage legalized prostitution?

4.   Does Millet accurately define and describe sex roles? Does she intend to? Does she assume a friendly or a hostile audience?

5.   What goals of the "Sexual Revolution" do you find most desirable? Least desirable?

The Politics of Housework

PAT MAINARDI

Liberated women—very different from women's liberation! The first signals all kinds of goodies, to warm the hearts (not to mention other parts) of the most radical men. The other signals—*housework*. The first brings sex without marriage, sex before marriage, cozy housekeeping arrangements ("You see, I'm living with this chick") and the self-content of knowing that you're not the kind of man who wants a doormat instead of a woman. That will come later. After all, who wants that old commodity anymore, the Standard American Housewife, all husband, home and kids. The New Commodity, the Liberated Woman, has sex a lot and has a Career, preferably something that can be fitted in with the household chores—like dancing, pottery, or painting.

On the other hand is women's liberation—and housework. What? You say this is all trivial? Wonderful! That's what I thought. It seemed perfectly reasonable. We both had careers, both had to work a couple of days a week to earn enough to live on, so why shouldn't we share the housework? So I suggested it to my mate and he agreed—most men are too hip to turn you down flat. "You're right," he said, "It's only fair."

Then an interesting thing happened. I can only explain it by stating that we women have been brainwashed more than even we can imagine. Probably too many years of seeing television women in ecstasy over their shiny waxed floors or breaking down over their dirty shirt collars. Men have no such conditioning. They recognize the essential fact of housework right from the very beginning. Which is that it stinks. Here's my list of dirty chores: buying groceries, carting them home and putting them away; cooking meals and washing dishes and pots; doing the laundry, digging out the place when things get out of control; washing floors. The list could go on but the sheer necessities are bad enough. All of us have to do these things, or get some one else to do them for us. The longer my husband contemplated these chores, the more repulsed he became, and so proceeded the change from the normally sweet considerate Dr. Jekyll into the crafty Mr. Hyde who would stop at nothing to avoid the horrors of—*housework.* As he felt himself backed into a corner laden with dirty dishes, brooms, mops, and reeking garbage, his front teeth grew longer and pointier, his fingernails haggled and his eyes grew wild. Housework trivial? Not on your life! Just try to share the burden.

So ensued a dialogue that's been going on for several years. Here are some of the high points:

"I don't mind sharing the housework, but I don't do it very well. We should each do the things we're best at."
Meaning: Unfortunately I'm no good at things like washing dishes or cooking. What I do best is a little light carpentry, changing light bulbs, moving furniture (*how often do you move furniture?*).
Also Meaning: Historically the lower classes (black men and us) have had hundreds of years experience doing menial jobs. It would be a waste of manpower to train someone else to do them now.
Also Meaning: I don't like the dull stupid boring jobs, so you should do them.

"I don't mind sharing the work, but you'll have to show me how to do it."
Meaning: I ask a lot of questions and you'll have to show me everything everytime I do it because I don't remember so good. Also don't try to sit down and read while I'm doing my jobs because I'm going to annoy hell out of you until it's easier to do them yourself.

"We used to be so happy!" (Said whenever it was his turn to do something.)
Meaning: I used to be so happy.

Meaning: Life without housework is bliss. (*No quarrel here. Perfect agreement.*)

"We have different standards, and why should I have to work to your standards. That's unfair."
Meaning: If I begin to get bugged by the dirt and crap I will say "This place sure is a sty" or "How can anyone live like this?" and wait for your reaction. I know that all women have a sore called "Guilt over a messy house" or "Household work is ultimately my responsibility." I know that men have caused that sore—if anyone visits and the place *is* a sty, they're not going to leave and say, "He sure is a lousy housekeeper." You'll take the rap in any case. I can outwait you.
Also Meaning: I can provoke innumerable scenes over the housework issue. Eventually doing all the housework yourself will be less painful to you than trying to get me to do half. Or I'll suggest we get a maid. She will do my share of the work. You will do yours. It's women's work.

"I've got nothing against sharing the housework, but you can't make me do it on your schedule."
Meaning: Passive resistance. I'll do it when I damned well please, if at all. If my job is doing dishes, it's easier to do them once a week. If taking out laundry, once a month. If washing the floors, once a year. If you don't like it, do it yourself oftener, and then I won't do it at all.

"I *hate* it more than you. You don't mind it so much."
Meaning: Housework is garbage work. It's the worst crap I've ever done. It's degrading and humiliating for someone of *my* intelligence to do it. But for someone of *your* intelligence . . .

"Housework is too trivial to even talk about."
Meaning: It's even more trivial to do. Housework is beneath my status. My purpose in life is to deal with matters of significance. Yours is to deal with matters of insignificance. You should do the housework.

"This problem of housework is not a man-woman problem! In any relationship between two people one is going to have a stronger personality and dominate."
Meaning: That stronger personality had better be *me*.

"In animal societies, wolves, for example, the top animal is usually a male even where he is not chosen for brute strength but on the basis of cunning and intelligence. Isn't that interesting?"

Meaning: I have historical, psychological, anthropological, and biological justification for keeping you down. How can you ask the top wolf to be equal?

"Women's liberation isn't really a political movement."

Meaning: The Revolution is coming too close to home.

Also Meaning: I am only interested in how *I* am oppressed, not how I oppress others. Therefore the war, the draft, and the university are political. Women's liberation is not.

"Man's accomplishments have always depended on getting help from other people, mostly women. What great man would have accomplished what he did if he had to do his own housework?"

Meaning: Oppression is built into the System and I, as the white American male receive the benefits of this System. I don't want to give them up.

Postscript

Participatory democracy begins at home. If you are planning to implement your politics, there are certain things to remember.

1. He *is* feeling it more than you. He's losing some leisure and you're gaining it. The measure of your oppression is his resistance.

2. A great many American men are not accustomed to doing monotonous repetitive work which never ushers in any lasting let alone important achievement. This is why they would rather repair a cabinet than wash dishes. If human endeavors are like a pyramid with man's highest achievements at the top, then keeping oneself alive is at the bottom. Men have always had servants (us) to take care of this bottom strata of life while they have confined their efforts to the rarefied upper regions. It is thus ironic when they ask of women— where are your great painters, statesmen, etc? Mme. Matisse ran a millinery shop so he could paint. Mrs. Martin Luther King kept his house and raised his babies.

3. It is a traumatizing experience for someone who has always thought of himself as being against any oppression or exploitation of one human being by another to realize that in his daily life he has been accepting and implementing (and benefiting from) this exploitation; that his rationalization is little different from that of the racist who says "Black people don't feel pain" (women don't mind doing the shitwork); and that the oldest form of oppression in

history has been the oppression of 50 per cent of the population by the other 50 per cent.

4. Arm yourself with some knowledge of the psychology of oppressed peoples everywhere, and a few facts about the animal kingdom. I admit playing top wolf or who runs the gorillas is silly but as a last resort men bring it up all the time. Talk about bees. If you feel really hostile bring up the sex of spiders. They have sex. She bites off his head.

The psychology of oppressed people is not silly. Jews, immigrants, black men, and all women have employed the same psychological mechanisms to survive: admiring the oppressor, glorifying the oppressor, wanting to be like the oppressor, wanting the oppressor to like them, mostly because the oppressor held all the power.

5. In a sense, all men everywhere are slightly schizoid—divorced from the reality of maintaining life. This makes it easier for them to play games with it. It is almost a cliché that women feel greater grief at sending a son off to war or losing him to that war because they bore him, suckled him, and raised him. The men who foment those wars did none of those things and have a more superficial estimate of the worth of human life. One hour a day is a low estimate of the amount of time one has to spend "keeping" oneself. By foisting this off on others, man gains seven hours a week—one working day more to play with his mind and not his human needs. Over the course of generations it is easy to see whence evolved the horrifying abstractions of modern life.

6. With the death of each form of oppression, life changes and new forms evolve. English aristocrats at the turn of the century were horrified at the idea of enfranchising working men—were sure that it signaled the death of civilization and a return to barbarism. Some working men were even deceived by this line. Similarly with the minimum wage, abolition of slavery, and female suffrage. Life changes but it goes on. Don't fall for any line about the death of everything if men take a turn at the dishes. They will imply that you are holding back the Revolution (their Revolution). But you are advancing it (your Revolution).

7. Keep checking up. Periodically consider who's actually *doing* the jobs. These things have a way of backsliding so that a year later once again the woman is doing everything. After a year make a list of jobs the man has rarely if ever done. You will find cleaning pots, toilets, refrigerators and ovens high on the list. Use time sheets if necessary. He will accuse you of being petty. He is above that sort of thing—

(housework). Bear in mind what the worst jobs are, namely the ones that have to be done every day or several times a day. Also the ones that are dirty—it's more pleasant to pick up books, newspapers etc. than to wash dishes. Alternate the bad jobs. It's the daily grind that gets you down. Also make sure that you don't have the responsibility for the housework with occasional help from him. "I'll cook dinner for you tonight" implies it's really your job and isn't he a nice guy to do some of it for you.

8. Most men had a rich and rewarding bachelor life during which they did not starve or become encrusted with crud or buried under the litter. There is a taboo that says that women mustn't strain themselves in the presence of men: we haul around 50 pounds of groceries if we have to but aren't allowed to open a jar if there is someone around to do it for us. The reverse side of the coin is that men aren't supposed to be able to take care of themselves without a woman. Both are excuses for making women do the housework.

9. Beware of the double whammy. He won't do the little things he always did because you're now a "Liberated Woman," right? Of course he won't do anything else either . . .

I was just finishing this when my husband came in and asked what I was doing. Writing a paper on housework. Housework? he said, *Housework?* Oh my god how trivial can you get. A paper on housework.

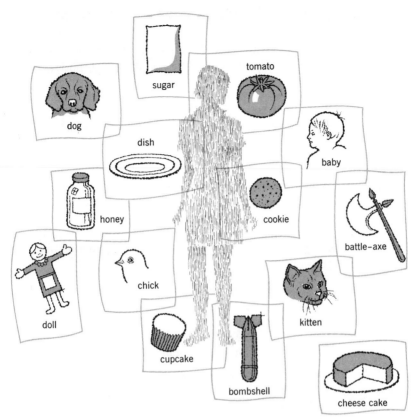

*What is in a name? Are names insulting or pleasing **because** they refer to real things? Do you find it strange that so many "female" terms of endearment are associated with food? What other categories of names are applied to women?*

Questions

1. Does the writer have a "typical" female point of view? How is the male point of view portrayed? Do you think the portrayal is accurate?

2. Is the lack of "cooperation" the writer finds in her domestic life representative of what occurs in most housekeeping situations? Does Mainardi fairly interpret the responses attributed to her husband?

3. Is housework as bad as Mainardi indicates it is? Are the domestic chores usually performed by men (such as mowing the lawn) "better" than such tasks as housecleaning?

4. Is the strategy of "statement" and "meaning" rhetorically effective in this essay?

5. Does Mainardi assume a sympathetic audience? Does she prepare for arguments against her case?

6. Can you think of any other aspects of the daily life of women or men which evoke images of entrapment or degradation?

7. Write a short, serious response to Mainardi's ideas either defending or attacking the fairness of having to do housework. Is a serious treatment likely to be more, or less, convincing than a humorous one? Why?

The Jailor

My night sweats grease his breakfast plate.
The same placard of blue fog is wheeled into position
With the same trees and headstones.
Is that all he can come up with,
The rattler of keys?

I have been drugged and raped.
Seven hours knocked out of my right mind
Into a black sack
Where I relax, foetus or cat,
Lever of his wet dreams.

Something is gone.
My sleeping capsule, my red and blue zeppelin,
Drops me from a terrible altitude.
Carapace smashed,
I spread to the beaks of birds.

O little gimlets!
What holes this papery day is already full of!
He has been burning me with cigarettes,

Pretending I am a Negress with pink paws.
I am myself. That is not enough.

The fever trickles and stiffens in my hair.
My ribs show. What have I eaten?
Lies and smiles.
Surely the sky is not that colour,
Surely the grass should be rippling.

All day, gluing my church of burnt matchsticks,
I dream of someone else entirely.
And he, for this subversion,
Hurts me, he
With his armoury of fakery.

His high, cold masks of amnesia.
How did I get here?
Indeterminate criminal,
I die with variety—
Hung, starved, burned, hooked!

I imagine him
Impotent as distant thunder,
In whose shadow I have eaten my ghost ration.
I wish him dead or away.
That, it seems is the impossibility,

That being free. What would the dark
Do without fevers to eat?
What would the light
Do without eyes to knife, what would he
Do, do, do without me?

Questions

1. Can you account for the poem's idea that marital sex is legalized rape? Do you suppose most wives regard their sexual relations as rape?

2. In what ways can a man be considered his wife's jailor? Can he force her to submit to him against her will? Can she force him to submit? Is the wife also her husband's jailor? Do male and female strategies differ in how to bring about the submission of the opposite sex? Do most people want others to submit to them? Does the poem assume that people have such desires? Are the fantasies expressed in the poem those of men or of women?

3. Does the poem represent a particular relationship, or a universal one? Do you feel that the writer is speaking to you, or is she trying to articulate a private situation?

Man As an Obsolete Life Form

BETSY WARRIOR

If men are going to destroy the planet Earth and all its inhabitants with violence and wars, all men should be killed, to preserve the rest of humankind. If they decide they don't want to keep on in the direction they're heading, they will have to control and subdue their inner nature as they have outer nature.

Like many other organisms in biological history, man has become an obsolete life form. He is an anachronism in this technological context. His muscles are no longer needed. The built-in obsolescence of his physical and emotional nature is now apparent.

The aggressive, destructive drives of man lack proper reasonable outlets. He is being phased out by technology. Sperm banks and test-tube babies can take over his last function, his only function that has positive effects for the human race. All the rest of his functions can be performed by females much more efficiently, minus the destruction.

In an agrarian society man could expend his energy tilling the land and caring for animals. In a hunting culture he consumed his energy fishing and killing animals. These special drives aren't needed now for survival; now they are an evolutionary hangover.

In the present era the same demands aren't existent. Now men consume their energy devising ways to kill, and killing each other.

Reprinted by permission of the author.

Their energy lacks outlet and makes man consume himself, like a frenzied shark eating his own guts. MAN HAS PASSED THE STAGE WHERE HE IS JUST UPSETTING THE BALANCE OF NATURE; HE IS THE IMBALANCE IN NATURE!

With the growing size of the human race, population control is necessary in some situations. But to consider only the quantity of the population, is to see only half the problem. The quality of the population is just as important to the future welfare and survival of the human race. Those who love war-games and destructive exercises to expend their energies are just as much of a threat to humanity as overpopulation.

The qualities of man make him unfit for life today. And like all harmful factors his life should come to an end. Due to great famines, plagues, and wars the population once had built-in checks. But that was a very miserable, cruel and inhumane way to insure the survival of some. The best didn't necessarily survive—only the most aggressive.

Today science has found ways to alleviate famine, conquer germs that cause plagues, and check the size of the population itself. One germ hasn't been identified and destroyed; the germ that causes war and destruction. That germ is man.

It is not in his interest to acknowledge his role in human suffering. The male has a vested interest in denying the implications and consequences of his existence, and that interest is the instinct of self-preservation. As long as man is in power he will never admit the necessity of his demise from the planet Earth for the achievement of a humane evolution.

The tyrannosaurus had to become extinct. Because of the dinosaurs' huge size and voracious appetite, other life forms were unable to develop and survive in its geological era. It needed all other life to feed on, to sustain its own life. After eating all other species it could use for food, it died of starvation. Only with their extinction at the end of the Cretaceous period, could other, better, life forms come into being and evolve.

Like the tyrannosaurus, man is blocking evolution and sustaining his life at the expense of other, better, life forms. Until he gives up existence, either voluntarily or by force, there will be no relief from suffering nor any moral progress on this planet.

In areas of the world more densely populated, certain species were driven out or became extinct for the protection of the population that replaced them. The more aggressive, predatory or competitive the creature, the more disruptive it was to the harmonious functioning of the culture.

A tiger on city streets would wreak havoc, and no one would think of keeping a shark in his swimming pool, though water is its natural habitat. Bears don't roam the parks, nor elephants stampede down the expressway. We can't live in harmony with these creatures, and about the only place a city dweller ever sees one of these animals is in the zoo.

In Africa where the land isn't so scarce, in relatively populated areas, preserves and parks are set aside to contain and restrict the movement of destructive species. They can roam and kill unrestrainedly within the limits of this preserve, but they are not allowed to subject the civilized to the consequences of their behavior, by infringing on their territory or peace of mind.

If all men with aggressive, homicidal or manipulative tendencies were restricted to one island or territory centuries ago, and had unrestricted freedom in these areas, they would have kept killing each other off, leaving the rest of the population in peace. Life would have evolved into something quite different from what it is today.

As things stand these types are dispersed throughout the population. They hold influential positions, and set a pattern for others to follow.

Killers aren't ostracized but honored. Soldiers, mercenaries, and policemen aren't the only ones who are given a license to kill. They are only the more overt types. Politicians and scientists among others also make death-dealing decisions.

In fact the great majority of the population is infected and accepts and endorses this behavior. Not confined by preserves, man's battleground is the world, and the whole population must suffer the consequences. No one is safe. Today man's weapons are too destructive, and the population too dense, to tolerate him in our midst.

If females feel some compunctions about eliminating him entirely, Man preserves and zoos might prove a rational alternative.

Betsy Warrior

Questions

1.   Examine the logic of the opening sentence. Why "all men"? Who would destroy them in the name of nonviolence? Is the opening sentence meant to be logical?

2.   Do *all* men "consume their energy devising ways to kill, and killing each other"? Do many men do this? Any women? Have opinion polls indicated much difference between men and women in attitudes to war and violence?

3.   Is the author's view of men one you know from personal experience? Does the author expect it to be? What assumptions does she make about her audience?

4.   How does the writer support her arguments? In what ways is this type of support convincing? Who would it be unlikely to convince?

5.   Could the writer be accused of having "aggressive, homicidal or manipulative tendencies" in this article? Is this a fair question? Is it a question more likely to be asked by a man than a woman?

6.   Write a parody of this article by adopting an even more extreme persona than "Betsy Warrior" and stretching your argument to such a degree that you use irony to make absurd the position you are supposedly defending.

The Feminine Mistake

HELEN LAWRENSON

You might have to go back to the Children's Crusade in 1212 A.D. to find as unfortunate and fatuous an attempt at manipulated hysteria as the Women's Liberation movement. For six months I have been reading their literature and listening to their strident speeches, and I had hoped that by now these sick, silly creatures would have huffed and puffed themselves out.

Instead, the movement is spreading, not only in America but in Europe; more and more women are letting themselves be worked up to a splenetic frenzy of hatred for men; and the latter, in cowardly panic lest they be labeled male chauvinists, are ignominiously making placatory noises. Male magazine editors, to a mouse, have jumped on the bandwagon, and every militant feminist with a typewriter is banging away on it. The books they produced last year sold so well that many bookstores have set up special Women's Lib sections in anticipation of increasing demand for the more than a dozen titles steaming off the presses this winter, with more to come, all contracted for by leading male publishers who fell over each other to compete for the authors. Last summer, the New York Shakespeare Festival put on a Women's Lib musical gawkishly entitled *Mod Donna*, written by two females and described as dealing with "women's sexual subjugation to Penis Power"; a group called

Reprinted by permission of Esquire Magazine © 1970 by Esquire, Inc.

the Feminist Repertory Theatre produced plays containing such fustian lines as "Have you made my body the incubator of your artificial passion?"; and actress Barbara Harris promised to direct a dramatic presentation of selected feminist writings from Susan B. Anthony on down, a theatrical event to be awaited with muted anticipation. The commercial lampreys of the cinema world will surely not be dilatory in latching on, just as they did with the youth revolution, so that before long we can expect to see a spate of films exploiting Women's Lib in different versions—comic, serious, sexy, and, of course, Cary Grant and Katharine Hepburn in the geriatric version.

It's a phony issue and a phony movement. Demands for equal political and legal rights, for child-care centers and equal pay for equal work are reasonable enough—although even in these areas some of the more belligerent feminists tend to go off the beam—but these have been submerged in a hair-raising emotional orgy of hatred as vicious as it is ludicrous, directed at love, marriage, children, the home, and encompassing en route, with wild catholicity, the penis, the Pill, false eyelashes, brassieres, Barbie dolls, Freud, Dr. Spock, the Old Left, the New Left, detergent advertisements, and such despicable male gallantries as opening doors for women and helping them on with their coats. What they are demanding is not equality but the absolute subjugation of men, or even their elimination.

These are not normal women. I think they are freaks. Besides, they are dead wrong in their assumption that most women detest men, marriage and housework so much that they can't wait to be liberated from them so they can rush out to work all day in factory, shop or office. Where do they get this lunatic idea that women had rather work for a boss than stay home and run their own domain? All orthodox Lib members seethe with bile at the thought of housework, to which they constantly refer as "shitwork," and rant continuously about the dreadful degradation of cooking meals, making beds, bathing babies. But the average normal woman derives a very basic happiness from performing these tasks. Most women have a strong nesting instinct and they *like* taking care of their homes. It may get tiresome at times but it sure as hell beats working. They get satisfaction from cooking special dishes to please their families, from polishing their best furniture and washing their grandmother's china, from planning new curtains or refurbishing an old chair. Even if they own nothing valuable or grand, what they have are Their Own Things and they enjoy taking care of them. Housework is not degrading, and there is nothing demeaning about caring for your home, your husband, your children. Besides, who do these Women's Lib characters think ought to do this "degrading" housework? Other women? Their husbands? One of them, Caroline Bird, in an article in *Signature,* the Diners Club magazine, suggests an end to the family system, which might be replaced by some sort of commune, and adds, "If women are totally liberated, more men and women would remain single," thus ignoring the fact that most women *want* to get married. Discussing the effect on industry, she writes, "The market for nursery furniture and child gear would taper off" (What? No more little pink or blue crib mattresses with bunnies and kittens on them?), and prophesies that "convenience foods" (whatever they are) and takeout-food shops would replace home-cooked meals and that "Home furnishings would give way to portable or disposable furniture." *Disposable furniture.* Can she really be kidding herself that this is what women want in their homes?

The worst thing about the movement is that it is distracting the attention of thousands of women from more urgent and important questions. They should get their priorities straight. Instead of yapping about men treating them as "sex objects" (and, personally, I have always *liked* being treated as a sex object), they might better devote themselves to more socially useful protests: against the war in Indochina, against nuclear, chemical and biological weapons, against environmental pollution, to name a few of the more obvious. Or the exploitation of migrant workers, the oppression of the blacks, the American Indians, the Alaskan Eskimos. Or any one of at least several hundred other projects more immediate and more deserving than the issue of whether or not women should do housework and let men whistle at them in the streets. There is only so much time and energy that each person has available to devote to causes. To try to persuade people to concentrate this time and energy on something as capricious and spurious as Women's Lib is not only wasteful but truly evil.

• • •

With a rare exception here and there, it is a movement of white, middle-class, college-educated women, and their appeal to the proletariat is minimal. In all their obsessive yammering about the injustice of not allowing women to do men's work, they aren't thinking of the average working-class jobs. No, these women have in mind bank presidents, Supreme Court justices, chairmen of the board or any other job which means Top Boss. (What they seem to ignore is that not all men can get these jobs, either.) They talk a lot about freeing working-class women from housework and, actually, women in different parts of the world have done just about everything at one time or another, but what woman in her right mind wants to go out and build subways or load cargo or mine coal? Nor do all women dream of becoming president of U.S. Steel (or even ambassador to Italy, so they can settle Trieste). Certainly not the average American woman, black or white. Rose Mary Byrd, a member of the Black Panthers, referring to Women's Lib groups, has said that while black men and women *together* are "fighting the whole power structure, those white chicks are talking about individual hang-ups like getting jobs"; and she added that "hating someone because he's a man is a way-out trip. . . . When they talk about myths of orgasm their minds are on the moon . . . the main thing they can't put up with is themselves."

That is exactly what they do talk about incessantly. Instructions on how to start a Women's Lib group in your own community advise you to get together eight to fifteen women who will meet once a week at each other's houses, presumably to discuss the iniquity of men. A topic should be selected for each week, and samples given include the questions: Why did you marry the man you did? What was your first sex experience? Do you pretend to have an orgasm?

· · ·

Women don't need [men] anyway, if you believe the Women's Lib leaders, whose views are made clear in the following quotes. Ti-Grace Atkinson: "Love has to be destroyed. It's an illusion that people care for each other." Abby Rockefeller: "Love between a man and a woman is debilitating and counterrevolutionary." Roxanne Dunbar: "Sex is just a commodity, a programmed activity. It is not a basic need." Miss Dunbar was the first Lib leader publicly to advocate the right for women to masturbate. (So who's stopping them?)

· · ·

American women have more freedom and more material advantages than any other women on earth. They are also notorious for their tendency to dominate their menfolk. As Dr. Spock remarked when he appeared on British television a few months ago, "If you liberate women in America one more inch, man will be completely subjugated." Sentiments like this have aroused the rage of Women's Lib groups: one of their publications portrayed him as a penis (obviously the most hateful object they could imagine) in a drawing, and a *Newsweek* journalist talking to Lib groups reported that they hissed at the mention of his name.

He was only confirming what many psychiatrists and sociologists have said previously. Dr. Theodore S. Weiss, formerly a senior psychiatrist of the New York City Department of Hospitals, once told me, "America is becoming a matriarchy." The American wife, he claimed, treats her husband as a combination of problem child and indentured servant. She expects him to be escort, meal ticket, handyman, errand boy and mother's helper. She is always trying to remodel and improve him. She supervises his manners and language, dictates how he shall dress, what friends he shall have, and how he shall spend his leisure time. Customarily, it is she who determines the decor of their home, the extent of their social orbit, and where they go on holidays. In public, she does not hesitate to interrupt him, contradict him, or attempt to regulate his habits. ("Don't give him any more to drink. He's had enough.") If he rebels, she nags him, bosses him, belittles him and tries to make him feel so inadequate that he would no more think of asserting his male authority as head of the family than he would dare wipe his hands on the guest towels in the bathroom. Increasingly, he suffers from nervous breakdowns, ulcers, premature heart attacks, insomnia, alcoholism. On the other hand, American women not only live longer than their men but they own more than fifty per cent of the money in the country, they have sixty-five per cent of the savings accounts, they control fifty-seven per cent of listed securities, have title to seventy-four per cent of suburban homes, and, according to The New York Sunday *Times,* control about eighty-seven and a half per cent of the total buying power.

So what are they bitching about? Careers? If a women is sufficiently ambitious, determined *and* gifted, there is practically nothing she can't do. We have been judges, legislators, bank presidents, college presidents, publishers, ambassadors, doctors, lawyers, scientists, Cabinet members, auditors, bond traders, tax experts, bullfighters, bartenders, plumbers, taxi drivers, riveters and even, some twenty-odd years ago, six per cent of the total number of the country's paperhangers. At the present time, we have a woman Director of the Mint, U.S. Treasurer, Chairman of the Federal Maritime Commission, as well as a couple of ambassadors. There is only one woman

Senator but ten women in the House. That there are not more of us in the top echelons is due to personal choice rather than denial of opportunity. The main life interest of the average woman quite simply lies in other directions: love, marriage, children, home. Men start work with the intention of working all their lives, often with the goal of rising to the top. The majority of women take their first jobs with the intention of working only until they get married, or, if they continue after marriage, until they have children. There are 29,500,000 women in the U.S. labor force today and those of that number who continue to work after marriage usually do so for reasons more economic than feminist. A Department of Labor questionnaire some years ago asked the motives of married women workers. The typical answer was: "Because my husband does not earn enough to support our family with the cost of living what it is." They did not say: "Because I'm just crazy about the factory assembly line."

There is, too, the matter of ability—or talent. (I'm not going into the question of genius here, although certainly the absence of any female equivalent to Beethoven, Shakespeare, Leonardo da Vinci or all the other great composers, writers and painters cannot be blamed on male oppression.) If women have it and are sufficiently dedicated to its advancement, they can make the grade. They do not always have it, or if they do, they sometimes lack the driving urge, the single-minded perseverance to exploit it. Furthermore, as far as politics go, whatever makes the feminists think that women could run the world any better than men? We got the vote, kiddo, and a fat lot of good we've done with it.

What they want is Everything—and they can't even agree on that. Although most of the groups who demonstrated last August on the fiftieth anniversary of the women's suffrage constitutional amendment listed free abortions among their demands, Women, Inc. of San Francisco, opposes abolition of the abortion laws, while Roxanne Dunbar, a leading Liberation spokeswoman, has been quoted as saying she feels support of abortion reform is "basically racist." Nor do they approve of the Pill, which they have denounced as "the final pollution, the exact analogue of DDT," or of douches —"another billion-dollar industry off our bodies"—while at the same time they attack the supposed hardships of motherhood. For years, feminists have railed against the sexual freedom of men and the double standard in morals, but now that the sexual revolution is here, they don't like it. Robin Morgan, a founder of W.I.T.C.H., is only one of those who claim that the new sexual freedom "never helped us—just made us more available," and someone else has written, "Women have gone from private property to public property—she's fair game." (This brings to mind the same question I had when I read Sally Kempton's statement, "In my adolescence, I screwed a lot of guys I didn't much like." Doesn't it ever occur to any of these girls that they can always say No?) Some of them are even against the newly acclaimed clitoral orgasm: "The hullabaloo over the female clitorally stimulated orgasm has further done nothing to liberate women because male domination of all women has not changed. Men are heard gloating over the power trip of 'I can make my girl go off like a machine gun.' "

To these women, a man is always wrong, no matter what. Although some feminists speak glowingly of the examples of communal nurseries and equality of work in Communist countries, others claim that "socialism in Cuba, China, the Soviet Union is a more advanced stage of male supremacy in which the means of production are owned by all men collectively." Many Lib members quit American radical groups because women had to type, answer telephones, run mimeograph machines and get coffee when what they thought they should have been doing, of course, was making the speeches and dictating the policy. As one of them has written, "The average student male wants a passive sex object . . . while he does all the fun things [like getting his head clubbed?] and bosses her around . . . he plays either big-shot male executive or Che Guevara—and he is my oppressor and my enemy." A manifesto issued on the West Coast by Redstockings refers to revolutionary groups as all "run by men and, consequently, interested in destroying us." Another complaint cites the "male supremacy rampant in white, male, anti-war groups" and says that women must "begin to demand control of these groups." (Note—not equal rights but *control.*)

Women like these will never be satisfied, no matter what rights they gain, because they are incapable of coming to terms with their own natures as females. Many of the Lib leaders are divorced or separated from their husbands (one deserted her husband and baby when the child was only one year old); many are childless; many more state flatly that they never want children or marriage. Those are their problems, but they should not try to impose them on other women, nor should they blame men for their own deficiencies. In nature, the basic, primary function of woman is to mate for the purpose of reproduction. Everything else has been superimposed, and women deny this at their peril. No matter what kind of political, economic or social setup we may have in the future, nothing is going to change the biological facts. Kate Millett can claim that gender identity is imposed by society, not genes, till she's blue in the face, but this doesn't make it true, as several anthropologists and psychiatrists have recently remarked. Even Simone de Beauvoir, top-drawer member of feminist hagiology, has written, "The division of the sexes is a biological fact, not an event in history." After treating us to a survey of the sex habits of ants, termites (did you know that a termite queen lays up to 4000 eggs a day? Well, now you do) and toads, she works her way up to birds, fishes and mammals and admits that "it is unquestionably the male who takes the female— she is *taken* . . . the male deposits his semen, the female receives." Even among female humans, she says, the "reproductive function is as important as the productive capacity." This doesn't mean that she approves of marriage or motherhood. Speaking with all the assurance of one who has experienced neither, she feels that "the tragedy of marriage is not that it fails to assure woman the promised happiness—there is no such assurance in regard to happiness—but that it mutilates her. . . . Real activities, real work, are the prerogative of her man . . . she is betrayed from the day he marries her." This contempt for the wife-mother role is as major a Women's Lib theme as hatred of men (the producer of a Lib radio program on New York's WBAI claimed that "to be a woman is to be nothing" and described the lives of housewives and mothers as "nothingness, total nothingness"). Simone thinks that marriage should be prohibited as a career for women. Man should free woman, she writes, and "give her something to *do* in the world" (a statement which could only have been written by a nullipara), although even she confesses that women enjoy marketing and cooking: "there is a poetry in making preserves . . . cooking is revelation and creation; and a woman can find special satisfaction in a successful cake." (She'd better retract that or they'll tear off all her buttons and drum her out of the movement.)

Women also dearly love cosmetics and it is idiotic for Lib members to say they should renounce them because they are degrading. Women enjoy using makeup, trying out new kinds, playing around with it. They always have, primarily to make themselves desirable in the eyes of men (a goal which is anathema to Lib members) and, secondarily, for the sheer pleasure of self-adornment. Women's Lib sneers at this and their members plaster stickers reading "This Ad

Insults Women" across posters which play up feminine sex appeal. It is an insult, they say, to assume that women are thinking of sex when they buy soap or perfume (Oh, but they are, honey) and in many cities Lib groups have publicly burned lipsticks, false eyelashes, bras and girdles, along with assorted objects like wedding certificates, birth-control pills, a Barbie doll and a book by Norman Mailer. (They lambaste Mailer and D. H. Lawrence as "male supremacist sexists," but have a kind word for Jean Genet.) The Barbie doll was included because they consider that "toys are, like abortion laws, deadly earnest instruments of women's oppression" dreamed up by fiendish male toy manufacturers who foist dolls, miniature stoves, refrigerators, mops and brooms on innocent and helpless little girl children. This, of course, is piffle. Little girls play with dolls, etc. because they love them, just as they love helping around the kitchen, dreaming of the day when they will be housewives and mothers, themselves. Why not? There is probably no career in the world as basically rewarding for a woman, from an emotional and psychological point of view as that of wife and mother. And what about love? Even the most emancipated career woman can fall in love; and love is not only when the bush becomes the burning bush, but it is also caring more about someone else than you do about yourself. When a woman falls madly in love with a man, she *wants* to wait on him and please him and be bossed by him and make a home for him and bear his children. Anyone who says otherwise is talking rubbish.

Women's Lib members who, for whatever personal reasons, find this idea loathsome are bucking nature. Women are the lunar sex. They do menstruate and they do have the babies. This is not the fault of men. It is asinine, as well as useless, to try to reverse the genders or to mount a venomous hate campaign against men for fulfilling the role for which nature made them. Men and women today should be working together to try to make the earth a better and a safer place. Any movement that tends to set them against each other by drumming up false sexual controversies is stupid and wrong. I cannot even feel sorry for these neurotic, inadequate women, because they are so appallingly selfish. They shriek about the monotony of housework with never a thought for the millions of men working their balls off at far more monotonous jobs in order to support their wives and children. Housework in America, despite all the labor-saving gadgets and easily prepared foods, may be boring at times, but it can't compare with the ego-destructive, soul-deadening boredom of standing in one spot on an assembly line, repeating one motion over and over, all day, every day.

Come off it, girls. Who is kidding whom? Besides, hasn't it ever dawned on you that whatever equality women get is given to them by men? So you see, no matter how you slice it, it's the same old sex game. Liberate me, daddy, eight to the bar.

First published in Esquire Magazine

Questions

1. Does the sex of the author affect your response to the article? This article originally appeared in *Esquire;* examine the various responses the same article might have provoked if it appeared in other periodicals such as *Good Housekeeping, Cosmopolitan, Vogue,* or *Ramparts,* written by a male author.

2. How would advocates of feminism respond to the accusation that they are not normal women, but freaks? What is "normal"? What is "freak"? Is calling someone a "freak" an effective rhetorical technique? An honest one?

3. Is the writer intentionally trying to polarize her audience? To overstate her case? Or simply to denounce something she sees as obviously wrong?

4. Does Lawrenson unfairly slight work such as abortion reform, to which many members of the woman's movement devote much of their energy?

5. What kinds of evidence does the author use to prove her charges against women's liberation? Is this evidence adequate? Does your response to this question depend on the preconceptions with which you read the article?

6. Is Lawrenson justified in suggesting that all feminists are trying to impose their problems on others and are trying to blame men for their own deficiencies?

7. What does the author mean when she says that "whatever equality women get is given to them by men"? Can equality be given? Do men have it in their power to grant equality?

8. Is the United States heading toward matriarchy? Would a matriarchy be a good thing? Is matriarchy the ideal of the woman's movement? Can claims that the U.S. is almost a matriarchy be reconciled with claims that women are strongly discriminated against?

9. Take any of the crucial issues debated by pro and anti women's liberation forces and write three separate long paragraphs using the same materials for each but altering language choices to fit the following positions: strongly for women's liberation, strongly against women's liberation, and "moderate" trying to sort out the "truth."

To All Black Women,
From All Black Men

Queen–Mother–Daughter of Africa
Sister of My Soul
Black Bride of My Passion
My Eternal Love

I greet you, my Queen, not in the obsequious whine of a cringing
Slave to which you have become accustomed, neither do I greet you
in the new voice, the unctuous supplications of the sleek Black
Bourgeoise, nor the bullying bellow of the rude Free Slave—but in
my own voice do I greet you, the voice of the Black Man. And although I greet you *anew,* my greeting is not *new,* but as old as the
Sun, Moon, and Stars. And rather than mark a new beginning, my
greeting signifies only my Return.

   I have Returned from the dead. I speak to you now from the
Here And Now. I was dead for four hundred years. For four hundred years you have been a woman alone, bereft of her man, a man-
less woman. For four hundred years I was neither your man nor
my own man. The white man stood between us, over us, around us.
The white man was your man and my man. Do not pass lightly over
this truth, my Queen, for even though the fact of it has burned
into the marrow of our bones and diluted our blood, we must bring

it to the surface of the mind, into the realm of knowing, glue our gaze upon it and stare at it as at a coiled serpent in a baby's playpen or the fresh flowers on a mother's grave. It is to be pondered and realized in the heart, for the heel of the white man's boot is our point of departure, our point of Resolve and Return—the blood-stained pivot of our future. (But I would ask you to recall, that before we could come up from slavery, we had to be pulled down from our throne.)

Across the naked abyss of negated masculinity, of four hundred years minus my Balls, we face each other today, my Queen. I feel a deep, terrifying hurt, the pain of humiliation of the vanquished warrior. The shame of the fleet-footed sprinter who stumbles at the start of the race. I feel unjustified. I can't bear to look into your eyes. Don't you know (surely you must have noticed by now: four hundred years!) that for four hundred years I have been unable to look squarely into your eyes? I tremble inside each time you look at me. I can feel . . . in the ray of your eye, from a deep hiding place, a long-kept secret you harbor. That is the unadorned truth. Not that I would have felt justified, under the circumstances, in taking such liberties with you, but I want you to know that I feared to look into your eyes because I knew I would find reflected there a merciless Indictment of my impotence and a compelling challenge to redeem my conquered manhood.

My Queen, it is hard for me to tell you what is in my heart for you today—what is in the heart of all my black brothers for you and all your black sisters—and I fear I will fail unless you reach out to me, tune in on me with the antenna of your love, the sacred love in ultimate degree which you were unable to give me because I, being dead, was unworthy to receive it; that perfect, radical love of black on which our Fathers thrived. Let me drink from the river of your love at its source, let the lines of force of your love seize my soul by its core and heal the wound of my Castration, let my convex exile end its haunted Odyssey in your concave essence which receives that it may give. Flower of Africa, it is only through the liberating power of your re-love that my manhood can be redeemed. For it is in your eyes, before you, that my need is to be justified, Only, only, only you and only you can condemn or set me free.

Be convinced, Sable Sister, that the past is no forbidden vista upon which we dare not look, out of a phantom fear of being, as the wife of Lot, turned into pillars of salt. Rather the past is an omni-scient mirror: we gaze and see reflected there ourselves and each other—what we used to be, what we are today, how we got this way, and what we are becoming. To decline to look into the Mirror of Then, my heart, is to refuse to view the face of Now.

I have died the ninth death of the cat, have seen Satan face to face and turned my back on God, have dined in the Swine's Trough, and descended to the uttermost echelon of the Pit, have entered the Den and seized my Balls from the teeth of a roaring lion!

Black Beauty, in impotent silence I listened, as if to a symphony of sorrows, to your screams for help, anguished pleas of terror that echo still throughout the Universe and through the mind, a million scattered screams across the painful years that merged into a single sound of pain to haunt and bleed the soul, a white-hot sound to char the brain and blow the fuse of thought, a sound of fangs and teeth sharp to eat the heart, a sound of moving fire, a sound of frozen heat, a sound of licking flames, a fiery-fiery sound, a sound of fire to burn the steel out of my Balls, a sound of Blue fire, a Bluesy sound, the sound of dying, the sound of my woman in pain, *the sound of my woman's pain,* THE SOUND OF MY WOMAN CALLING ME, ME, I HEARD HER CALL FOR HELP, I HEARD THAT MOURNFUL SOUND BUT HUNG MY HEAD AND FAILED TO HEED IT, I HEARD MY WOMAN'S CRY, I HEARD MY WOMAN'S SCREAM, I HEARD MY WOMAN BEG THE BEAST FOR MERCY, I HEARD HER BEG FOR ME, I HEARD MY WOMAN BEG THE BEAST FOR MERCY FOR ME, I HEARD MY WOMAN DIE, I HEARD THE SOUND OF HER DEATH, A SNAPPING SOUND, A BREAKING SOUND, A SOUND THAT SOUNDED FINAL, THE LAST SOUND, THE ULTIMATE SOUND, THE SOUND OF DEATH, ME, I HEARD, I HEAR IT EVERY DAY, I HEAR HER NOW . . . I HEAR YOU NOW . . . I HEAR YOU. . . . I heard you then . . . your scream came like a searing bolt of lightning that blazed a white streak down my black back. In a cowardly stupor, with a palpitating heart and quivering knees, I watched the Slaver's lash of death slash through the opposing air and bite with teeth of fire into your delicate flesh, the black and tender flesh of African Motherhood, forcing the startled Life untimely from your torn and outraged womb, the sacred womb that cradled primal man, the womb that incubated Ethiopia and populated Nubia and gave forth Pharaohs unto Egypt, the womb that painted the Congo black and mothered Zulu, the womb of Mero, the womb of the Nile, of the Niger, the womb of Songhay, of Mali, of Ghana, the womb that felt the might of Chaka before he saw the Sun, the Holy Womb, the womb that knew the future form of Jomo Kenyatta, the womb of

Mau Mau, the womb of the blacks, the womb that nurtured Toussaint L'Ouverture, that warmed Nat Turner, and Gabriel Prosser, and Denmark Vesey, the black womb that surrendered up in tears that nameless and endless chain of Africa's Cream, the Black Cream of the Earth, that nameless and endless black chain that sank in heavy groans into oblivion in the great abyss, the womb that received and nourished and held firm the seed and gave back Sojourner Truth, and Sister Tubman, and Rosa Parks, and Bird, and Richard Wright, and your other works of art who wore and wear such names as Marcus Garvey and DuBois and Kwame Nkrumah and Paul Robeson and Malcolm X and Robert Williams, and the one you bore in pain and called Elijah Muhammad, but most of all that nameless one they tore out of your womb in a flood of murdered blood that splashed upon and seeped into the mud. And Patrice Lumumba, and Emmett Till, and Mack Parker.

O, My Soul! I became a sniveling craven, a funky punk, a vile, groveling bootlicker, with my will to oppose petrified by a cosmic fear of the Slavemaster. Instead of inciting the Slaves to rebellion with eloquent oratory, I soothed their hurt and eloquently sang the Blues! Instead of hurling my life with contempt into the face of my Tormentor, *I shed your precious blood!* When Nat Turner sought to free me from my Fear, my Fear delivered him up unto the Butcher—a martyred monument to my Emasculation. My spirit was unwilling and my flesh was weak. Ah, eternal ignominy!

I, the Black Eunuch, divested of my Balls, walked the earth with my mind locked in Cold Storage. I would kill a black man or woman quicker than I'd smash a fly, while for the white man I would pick a thousand pounds of cotton a day. What profit is there in the blind, frenzied efforts of the (Guilty!) Black Eunuchs (Justifiers!) who hide their wounds and scorn the truth to mitigate their culpability through the pallid sophistry of postulating a Universal Democracy of Cowards, pointing out that in history no one can hide, that if not at one time then surely at another the iron heel of the Conqueror has ground into the mud the Balls of Everyman? Memories of yesterday will not assuage the torrents of blood that flow today from my crotch. Yes, History could pass for a scarlet text, its jot and tittle graven red in human blood. More armies than shown in the books have planted flags on foreign soil leaving Castration in their wake. But no Slave should die a natural death. There is a point where Caution ends and Cowardice begins. Give me a bullet through the brain from the gun of the beleaguered oppressor on the night of siege. Why is there dancing and singing in the Slave Quarters? A Slave who dies of natural causes cannot balance two dead flies in the Scales of Eternity. Such a one deserves rather to be pitied than mourned.

Black woman, without asking how, just say that we survived our forced march and travail through the Valley of Slavery, Suffering, and Death—there, that Valley there beneath us hidden by that drifting mist. Ah, what sights and sounds and pain lie beneath that mist! And we had thought that our hard climb out of that cruel valley led to some cool, green and peaceful, sunlit place—but it's all jungle here, a wild and savage wilderness that's overrun with ruins.

But put on your crown, my Queen, and we will build a New City on these ruins.

Questions

1. How does the "inside address" help establish audience expectations? Why does Cleaver adopt the form of a letter and rely on "you" and "I" throughout?

2. What does Cleaver mean by "the voice of the Black Man"? Does Cleaver present a distinctly "masculine" argument?

3. Is this article written for men as well as for women? How would the militant members of the woman's movement react to Cleaver's ideas? Would other women react differently?

4. Why are manhood and masculinity important to Cleaver? What part do they play in the Black liberation struggle? Why is Black Womanhood important for Black Manhood? Black Manhood for Black Womanhood?

5. What role does Cleaver expect the Black Woman to fulfill?

6. Characterize the voice Cleaver adopts in this article. How does it differ from other male voices in this anthology? From the female voices? Might a woman write in Cleaver's voice?

7. What is the effect of Cleaver's use of italics, capitals, and ellipses? Try breaking up a few of Cleaver's sentences according to the conventions of modern poetry. Is this "article" a "poem"?

8. Use Cleaver's style as a model for a "letter" to women or to men making clear your attitude toward the ways members of the opposite sex help you define your own feelings of masculinity or femininity.